BusinessManagement DAILY

SURPRISE TAX WINDFALL FOR SMALL BUSINESS OWNERS

AUTHORS
Ken Berry, Bill Bischoff, CPA

EDITORS
Robert Lentz

INTERIOR DESIGN
Michelle Peña

EDITORIAL DIRECTOR
Patrick DiDomenico

ASSOCIATE PUBLISHER
Adam Goldstein

PUBLISHER
Phillip A. Ash

© 2020, 2019, 2018. 2017, 2016, 2014, 2013, 2012, 2011, 2010, 2009, 2008. Business Management Daily, a division of Capitol Information Group, Inc., 7600A Leesburg Pike, West Building, Suite 300, Falls Church, VA 22043-2004. Phone: (800) 543-2055; www.BusinessManagementDaily.com. All rights reserved. No part of this report may be reproduced in any form or by any means without written permission from the publisher. Printed in U.S.A.

ISBN 9781796443424 (11th edition)

This publication is designed to provide accurate and authoritative information regarding the subject matter covered. It is sold with the understanding that the publisher is not engaged in rendering legal or financial service.

Contents

Introduction

Far too many people sit around and wait for promised tax reform in the hope that politicians will give them a tax break. The Internal Revenue Service counts on taxpayers to assume that kind of passive attitude. What the government doesn't like are take-charge, active taxpayers who make their own tax breaks. Such people cost the IRS big money because they learn how to slash their own taxes.

That's the purpose of this special report, which includes the key tax law changes over the past several years. It covers dozens of IRS-approved tax-reduction strategies that can save you thousands of dollars. I can practically guarantee that if you put these ideas to good use, you'll achieve significant tax savings and find innovative (and perfectly legal) ways to shelter investment income and sidestep tax traps.

Remember, too, that your tax savings don't end this year. They will endure, year after year, if you continue to take a proactive role in tax-trimming strategies.

PHILLIP A. ASH, CPA
Publisher
Small Business Tax Strategies

1. Begin With Best Tax-Free Devices

Almost four decades ago, Ronald Reagan had just been elected, the economy was recuperating from one recession and dipping into yet another, and Washington delivered one of the biggest overall tax cuts ever in the Economic Recovery Tax (ERTA) Act of 1981. Soon after, sweeping changes for individual taxpayers were included in another major tax law, the Tax Reform Act (TRA) of 1986.

In the intervening years, Congress has passed dozens of new tax laws, with a mixed bag of results. Significantly, the massive Economic Growth and Tax Relief Reconciliation Act of 2001 (EGTRRA) created a bevy of

new tax breaks for individuals, businesses and estates. But many favorable provisions in that law were scheduled to "sunset" after 2010.

Subsequently, new economic stimulus laws such as the American Recovery and Reinvestment Act of 2009 (ARRA) and the Small Business Jobs Act of 2010 provided tax-saving opportunities for individuals and small business owners. Next, the 2010 Tax Relief Act (formally the Tax Relief, Unemployment Insurance Reauthorization and Job Creation Act) preserved tax rate cuts for investors, extended various other provisions and revamped the estate tax law through the end of 2012. The American Taxpayer Relief Act of 2012 (ATRA) extended many of these provisions and modified others. Then the Tax Increase Prevention Act of 2014 (TIPA) extended most provisions that had expired again, but only for 2014. Soon after, the Protecting Americans from Tax Hikes (PATH) Act of 2015 retroactively restored almost all these provisions to 2015, making many of them permanent, with certain modifications.

Notably, Congress then passed the Tax Cuts and Jobs Act (TCJA) of 2017, the largest overhaul of the tax code since the days of the Reagan administration. Although the TCJA cuts taxes for individuals while eliminating certain tax breaks for 2018 and thereafter, the main provisions for individuals are scheduled to sunset after 2025.

Finally, a new spending measure passed at the end of 2019, the Further Consolidated Appropriations Act, includes a number of tax extenders, new disaster relief and significant retirement-based provisions under the "Setting Every Community Up for Retirement Enhancement (SECURE)" Act, among other changes.

Make way for the Tax Cuts and Jobs Act

The Tax Cuts and Jobs Act (TCJA) was the most sweeping tax legislation in more than 30 years. Generally, the changes are scheduled to sunset after 2025, while most business provisions are permanent. Some of the key provisions in the TCJA affecting individual taxpayers are as follows:

- Individual tax rates are cut. The new tax rate structure features a top tax rate of 37%.
- The standard deduction is essentially doubled to $12,000 for single filers and $24,000, subject to indexing ($12,400 and $24,800 for 2020, respectively). As a result of these changes and modifications for itemized deductions, many taxpayers who have itemized in the past will now claim the standard deduction instead.
- Personal exemptions, including exemptions for dependents, are eliminated.

- The child tax credit (CTC) is increased from $1,000 to $2,000, of which $1,400 is refundable.
- The deduction for mortgage interest is revised by lowering the threshold for interest paid on new acquisition debt from $1 million to $750,000 and eliminating the deduction for interest paid on home equity debt.
- The deduction for state and local taxes (SALT), including (1) property taxes and (2) income or sales taxes, is limited to $10,000 annually.
- The threshold for deducting medical expenses is reduced from 10% of adjusted gross income (AGI) to 7.5% of AGI. Initially, the reduced threshold only applied to 2017 and 2018 under the TCJA. However, the 2019 spending law extends this tax break through 2020.
- The deduction for charitable donations is preserved and the annual limit for the deduction for monetary contributions is increased from 50% of AGI to 60%.
- Deductions for miscellaneous expenses, casualty and theft losses (except for disaster area losses), job-related moving expenses (except for active duty military), alimony deductions (for agreements after 2018), business entertainment expenses and domestic production activity expenses are eliminated.
- The exemption amounts for the alternative minimum tax (AMT), as well as the thresholds for phasing out the AMT exemption amounts, are raised.
- Use of funds in Section 529 is expanded to include up to $10,000 of qualified K-12 tuition expenses in public, private and religious schools.
- The rule allowing recharacterizations of Roth IRA conversions is repealed.
- The rule allowing tax-free exchanges of like-kind properties is limited to exchanges of real estate properties.

- The estate tax exemption is doubled from $5 million to $10 million (indexed to $11.58 million in 2020).

- The individual insurance mandate under the Affordable Care Act (ACA) is abolished after 2018.

Some of the key provisions affecting small businesses in the TCJA are as follows:

- The corporate tax structure, with a top rate of 35%, is replaced with a flat 21% rate.

- The maximum Section 179 allowance is doubled from $500,000 to $1 million and the phase-out threshold is raised from $2 million to $2.5 million, subject to indexing ($1.2 million and $2.55 million for 2019,

respectively).

- Bonus depreciation is increased from 50% to 100% for a five-year period before gradually being phased out over the following five years.

- The deduction limits for luxury cars are raised substantially. For instance, the maximum first-year deduction is increased to $10,000.

- The rules for depreciating certain leasehold improvements over a 15-year recovery period are consolidated.

- A new deduction of up to 20% of qualified business income (QBI) is created for pass-through entities and sole proprietors.

- The deduction for business interest

Contribution limits for salary-reduction accounts and IRAs

Tax year	401(k), 403(b) and 457 plans	SIMPLE plan	IRAs (including Roths)*
2009–2011	16,500	11,500	5,000
2012	17,000	11,500	5,000
2013–2014	17,500	12,000	5,500
2015–2017	18,000	12,500	5,500
2018	18,500	12,500	5,500
2019	19,000	13,000	6,000
2020	19,500	13,500	6,000

If you're age 50 or older ...

The 2001 tax law allows some taxpayers to play catch-up with larger contributions. For people age 50 or over, the maximum contributions, including catch-up contributions, are:

Tax year	401(k), 403(b) and 457 plans	SIMPLE plan	IRAs (including Roths)*
2009–2011	22,000	14,000	6,000
2012	22,500	14,000	6,000
2013–2014	23,000	14,500	6,500
2015–2017	24,000	15,500	6,500
2018	24,500	15,500	6,500
2019	25,000	16,000	7,000
2020	26,000	16,500	7,000

*If married, each spouse can contribute the listed amounts to his or her own IRA.

expenses is capped at 30% (except for qualified small businesses).

- Deductions for qualified transportation benefits are repealed.
- The deduction for domestic production activity expenses is repealed.
- The deduction for business entertainment expenses is repealed.
- The corporate AMT is repealed.
- A new deduction of up to 25% of family and medical leave wages is created, now extended by the 2019 spending law to 2020.
- The rules for net operating loss (NOL) carryforwards and carrybacks are revised.
- The cash accounting method is available to more qualified small businesses.
- The system of international taxation is completely revamped.

Remember that the changes for individuals generally are scheduled to sunset after 2025, but Congress could extend certain provisions beyond that date or reinstate prior provisions even sooner. The tax law is continuously evolving.

Keep accurate records

For starters, you can't cut your taxes unless you can prove that your deductions and income exclusions are legitimate. Whether it's a business lunch attended by your spouse or wages paid to the kids, precise records are key to backing up any write-offs.

But you don't need to compile an encyclopedia to satisfy the IRS. Just use an appointment book or a day planner, and then, each evening, record every activity that might affect your taxes.

For instance, if Jeff pays his 16-year-old daughter to pick up a printer cartridge, he should note it, along with the time his daughter spent working. Or, if Linda pays for her meals while on a business trip, she should record the details.

Also, remember to keep all your receipts. When it comes time to fill out your tax return, these will allow you to take every deduction to which you're entitled.

Recommendation: Traditionally, the IRS has closely examined travel and entertainment (T&E) expenses. The best way to document business use of a car is by keeping a log in your car's glove box or on a spreadsheet. Or use your personal calendar at tax time to reconstruct business trips and mileage. But note that entertainment expenses aren't deductible after 2017.

Make capital gain taxes disappear on profitable home sales

Possibly the biggest tax break on the books: For sales of principal residences, gains of up to $500,000 ($250,000 for single filers and married filing separately) are tax-free. Even better, homeowners can "recycle" this generous break every two years. The exclusion doesn't apply, however, to the extent of any depreciation claimed after May 6, 1997 (for example, due to an office in the home or rental of the property).

To qualify for the exclusion, you must own and use the home as your main residence at least two out of the five years preceding the sale. But failure to meet this holding-period rule doesn't completely eliminate the exclusion as long as the sale is forced by a job change, health reasons or certain other unforeseen circumstances.

In this situation, the normal gain exclusion limit is prorated based on the actual period of ownership and use divided by two years. For example, if a single person must sell her house after only one year due to a job transfer, the exclusion is $125,000, or half the normal amount [$250,000 x (1-year holding period/2-year requirement)].

The prorated exclusion rule also applies if the individual sells the home within two years of an earlier sale for which gain was excluded. Again, the second sale must be necessitated by a job change, health reasons or unforeseen circumstances.

When a couple gets married and they own separate residences, each is entitled to a $250,000 gain exclusion, assuming both meet the other qualification rules for each home. For

Estate tax exemption amounts

Tax year	Single	Married
2009	3,500,000	7,000,000
2010*	unlimited	unlimited
2011	5,000,000	10,000,000
2012	5,120,000	10,240,000
2013	5,250,000	10,500,000
2014	5,340,000	10,680,000
2015	5,430,000	10,860,000
2016	5,450,000	10,900,000
2017	5,490,000	10,980,000
2018	11,180,000	22,360,000
2019	11,400,000	22,800,000
2020	11,580,000	23,600,000

*Can elect $5 million exemption.

example, if the couple moves into the husband's home, the wife can sell her house and exclude $250,000 as long as she owned it and used it as her residence for at least two out of the five preceding years.

What if the couple then decides to sell the husband's home? He will also be eligible for the full $250,000 exclusion if he meets the same test, even if his sale occurs less than two years after the wife's transaction.

The same would be true if the wife sold her home and excluded the gain shortly before the marriage. If the couple chooses to reside in the husband's home, they become eligible for the $500,000 joint-filer exclusion after more than two years have passed since the wife excluded gain from the sale of her former home. (Interestingly enough, the law defines a "principal residence" liberally if it meets the two-of-five-years test. Boats, motor homes, house trailers and the like can qualify for the gain exclusion.)

If you and your spouse are considering buying a "fixer upper" in a desirable neighbor-hood, the potential tax savings are enticing. You can live in the house for two years, complete the renovation and wind up paying no federal taxes on gains up to $500,000. Then you can buy another house and do it all over again.

However, be aware of a recent tax crackdown. Under a 2008 housing act, appreciation on a principal residence attributable to nonqualified use after 2008 is not eligible for the gain exclusion for sales realized after 2008. Nonqualified use includes use as a vacation home or rental property. The portion attributable to non-qualified use is determined on a pro rata basis.

Example: Mark and Laura, a married couple, bought a house on Jan. 1, 2017, for $500,000. After using it as a vacation home for three years, they move into the house as their principal residence for two years and then sell it for $1 million.

Previously, Mark and Laura could exclude the entire $500,000 gain from tax. Under the tax law crackdown, 60% of the use (three years out of five years) counts as nonqualified use. Thus, only 40% of the gain—or $200,000—qualifies for the gain exclusion.

Fund retirement plans to the max

From a tax point of view, there's no doubt where an individual's first investment dollars should go: into a tax-deferred retirement plan. This might be a pension or profit-sharing plan, including a 401(k) plan, through your employer or a Keogh, SEP or solo 401(k) plan if you're self-employed. Or, it can be an Individual Retirement Account (IRA) if (1) neither you nor your spouse is eligible for a qualified retirement plan or (2) you're eligible for another plan but your adjusted gross income (AGI) is less than the phaseout thresholds.

Such retirement plans offer a pure tax shelter. Up to specific limits, you can receive a full write-off for every dollar contributed. A taxable income of $100,000, for example, may be instantly reduced to $95,000 with a $5,000 contribution to a retirement plan.

What's more, money inside the retirement

plan will compound, free of income taxes. Say Elaine invests $5,000 in a Treasury bond paying 5%. That's $250 per year. However, if she is in the top 37% tax bracket, she'll have to pay $92.50 in federal income taxes, leaving her only $5,157.50 to reinvest the second year. Inside a retirement plan, she'll have $5,250 to reinvest. Over time, the difference can be substantial. Elaine won't have to pay income tax until she takes money out of the retirement plan.

If you qualify, you may also contribute $6,000 to a Roth IRA every year ($12,000 for married couples); these are the limits for 2020. As we'll explain in Chapter 4, Roth IRA contributions aren't deductible, but earnings accumulate tax-free and can eventually be withdrawn tax-free.

The ability to contribute to a Roth IRA, however, is subject to phaseout rules if your adjusted gross income for 2020 exceeds a $124,000 threshold ($196,000 if married).

Take advantage of higher contribution limits for retirement plans

EGTRRA included one of the biggest batches of retirement savings incentives ever. Individuals can now make larger deductible contributions to virtually all types of tax-deferred retirement accounts. Bigger contribution limits also apply to employer-sponsored plans such as 401(k) and profit-sharing arrangements, as well as self-employed plans (like Keoghs and SEPs), traditional IRAs and tax-free Roth IRAs. *(See table on page 3.)* Another incentive: The tax act permits individuals age 50 and older to make additional "catch-up contributions" over the expanded limits that apply to everybody else.

Estate tax: How to 'disinherit' Uncle Sam today

Ever since 2001, the "sunset" provisions in EGTRRA placed estate planning under a cloud. But subsequent legislation eventually provided greater clarity. Under EGTRRA, the federal estate tax exemption gradually increased, while the top estate tax rate decreased *(see box on page 5).* In 2009, the estate tax exemption effectively sheltered $3.5 million of assets from federal estate tax. If assets totaled $3.5 million or less, no estate tax was due. If assets added up to $3.6 million, estate tax was owed only on $100,000. In a 45% tax bracket, that's a $45,000 tax obligation.

Then the estate tax was completely repealed for 2010. Initially, it was scheduled to return in 2011 under less favorable conditions. However, beginning in 2011, the 2010 Tax Relief Act provided temporary relief in the form of a $5 million exemption per individual. Also, for a decedent dying in 2010, an executor could elect to use the rules in effect for 2011. ATRA extended the $5 million exemption (indexed for inflation each year) on a permanent basis. Finally, the TCJA doubled the exemption to $10 million, indexed for inflation each year.

What's more, the $10 million exemption ($11.58 million for 2020) is "portable." So, a married couple can currently leave up to $23.16 million to their children tax-free.

Example: Jim and Virginia, a married couple with two children, own $20 million in assets. For simplicity, we'll assume the value of their assets remains the same over time.

Jim dies early in 2020 and leaves $6 million to their children ($3 million each) and $4 million to Virginia. The $6 million bequest to the children is sheltered by the estate tax exemption for Jim's estate, and the $4 million bequest to Virginia is sheltered by the unlimited marital deduction. Virginia dies later in 2020 and leaves the remaining $14 million to the two children ($7 million each). The entire transfer is sheltered from estate tax by the exemption for her estate ($11.58 million for 2020) and the $5.58 million balance of the estate tax exemption for Jim's estate.

If a surviving spouse is predeceased by more than one spouse, the portable exclusion available to the surviving spouse is limited to the lesser of $10 million indexed for inflation ($11.58 million for 2020) or the unused exclusion of the last-deceased spouse.

Find tax shelters that still work

What if you've maxed out on the available retirement plans but still want more tax shelter? What else can you do?

Back in 1986, the TRA eliminated many classic tax shelters, as well as providing limits on losses from passive activities. A few tax shelters are left, however, in real estate and oil and gas, which can reduce the taxes that you'll owe on earned income or investment income:

- **Directly owned real estate.** If you own investment property, singly or as part of a group, you may be able to deduct your losses.

- **Low-income housing.** Investors provide money for low-rent apartments occupied by the working poor and the elderly. (These are not no-income welfare projects.) Owners may make money on the property's appreciation and from the tax credits.

- **Oil and gas drilling.** If you think that oil prices will continue to increase in the next few years, you may want to speculate in a drilling partnership. Drilling fund investors can qualify for a special upfront tax break: the deduction for intangible drilling costs. A dollar invested this year might provide a deduction of 50 cents, 70 cents or even 90 cents this year.

To get the write-off, though, you can't hide behind a limited liability shield during drilling. So you should look for a general partnership that has ample insurance, in case of any drilling disasters.

Many partnerships let you elect limited partnership status after the drilling is completed—a maneuver that the IRS has approved.

Even a 90% deduction, in the top 37% tax bracket for a high-income taxpayer, saves only 33 cents. You still have 67 cents "in the deal."

Thus, it's advisable to invest only if you believe oil prices will rise and pick a general partner with a record of making cash distributions to investors.

Make the most of tax-free investment income

- **Roth IRA earnings and gains.** Income earned on Roth IRA account balances can be withdrawn tax-free after the account has been open more than five years and the participant is at least age 59½.

- **Municipal bonds.** Interest is tax exempt, not just tax deferred.

- **In-state municipal bonds.** These can deliver interest that's exempt from state and local income taxes, too.

- **Muni bond funds.** Required investment may be only a few hundred dollars, yet investors enjoy professional bond selection and diversification. Some funds hold only in-state munis.

- **Tax-free money market funds.** These funds hold munis that mature in a year or less, so there's no fluctuation of principal and no federal income tax.

- **Life insurance.** With permanent life insurance, cash value builds free of income taxes. You can tap the cash value via tax-free policy loans.

- **Variable life insurance.** The insured can invest cash value in stock funds and many other types of investments, in the hope of higher returns.

- **Deferred annuities.** As with life insurance, the investor enjoys tax-free buildup. However, it costs to take out the money.

- **Equipment leasing income funds.** These funds buy business equipment (rail cars, computers, marine containers and so forth) and lease them to users. Depreciation shelters the leasing income.

Play tax-bracket arbitrage

Many tax-reduction strategies involve shifting income to lower tax brackets. Even with the top federal tax bracket of 37% in 2020, some executives and professionals are in an effective tax bracket close to 50% or possibly even higher because of other income tax provisions, including the 3.8% of Medicare surtax on investment income, the rules on employment taxes, plus state and local income taxes.

Therefore, it makes sense for high-income taxpayers to shift income to those who are in the 10% or 12% bracket, or even a zero tax bracket, such as their kids or retired parents. If you've set up an S corporation, trust or partnership, you may be able to allocate some income to one of them.

Build wealth with this 'family device'

If you run an unincorporated business or a small corporation, you can split income among your children or other family members in lower tax brackets. The net result: The family will enjoy larger after-tax income from the same amount of business income.

For unincorporated businesses, a taxpayer could establish a family partnership and then give partnership interests to low-bracket family members. In the case of a small corporation, he could elect "S corporation" status and then give the shares to family members.

In 2020, you can give up to $15,000 worth of assets to each family member without any adverse gift tax consequences. Also, a married couple can jointly give a total of $30,000 worth of assets to each recipient. Beyond the $15,000/ $30,000 exemption, each spouse could bequeath $11.58 million worth of assets in 2020, tax-free, at death. However, if they gave away large amounts during their lifetimes, they would use up all or part of this $11.58 million unified estate and gift tax exemption per spouse.

The family partnership technique works well for some taxpayers, but it has disadvantages. You can't use it for a personal service business, for example. Plus, all the partners have considerable legal rights. Perhaps most important, the IRS takes a hard look at all family partnerships.

Thus, instead you may prefer to incorporate a business and elect S corporation status. Most businesses can make this election. Majority shareholders retain control of the company, including the decision on how much business cash flow to distribute.

Note also that the TCJA creates a new up-to-20% deduction on "qualified business income" (OBI) of pass-through entities and sole proprietorships, beginning in 2018. This deduction is subject to phase-outs under a complex set of rules *(see Chapter 3)*.

2. Dig Deep for Every Deduction Below the Surface

To the old adage about two sure things in life—death and taxes—we can add a couple of more points. One, the federal government will never stop tinkering with the tax code. Two, tax law isn't simple. Each law contains hundreds, even thousands, of pages of impenetrable prose along with confusing IRS "guidelines."

In far too many cases, the effect is intimidation. Taxpayers, and even some tax professionals, don't know what deductions are allowed, so they decide to play it safe and bypass legitimate deductions.

If you understand what's buried in those tax laws, however, you'll know how far you can go without running into the IRS wall. You can aggressively take advantage of every tax break that applies to you, with little or no audit risk. Although Congress is constantly revising its tax-collection system, including the latest sweeping changes in the TCJA, it's still possible to lock in many money-saving strategies. But you have to know what they are, how to take them and how to protect yourself from an IRS audit. And most important, you have to take immediate action.

Convert your hobby expenses into deductible expenses

Do you collect coins or baseball cards, do needlepoint, breed horses and so forth? Under current tax rules, you get no deduction for your hobby expenses or other miscellaneous expenses.

For instance, if you make a quilt and sell it for $500, you can no longer deduct the $500 of expenses incurred in quilt-making as you could prior to the TCJA. However, if you report a profit in three out of five consecutive years, the activity is presumed to NOT be a hobby, so you may be able to deduct all the reasonable business-related expenses, even if they create an overall tax loss. (For horse breeding or racing, you would need to show a profit in only two out of seven consecutive years.)

Under the TCJA, the deduction for miscellaneous expenses is eliminated for 2018 through 2025. It is scheduled to be resurrected in 2026.

Write off home computer, furnishings

Many self-employed taxpayers can deduct equipment purchases, rather than capitalizing them, under Section 179 of the tax code. The Section 179 deduction applies to most business assets, including home office computers and furniture.

The maximum Section 179 deduction has been raised several times in this century. Recently, under the Small Business Jobs Act of 2010, the maximum deduction was increased from $250,000 to $500,000 for tax years beginning in 2010 and 2011. Then ATRA and TIPA preserved a maximum $500,000 for 2012 through 2014. Subsequently, the PATH Act made the maximum $500,000 deduction permanent, beginning in 2015. Finally, the TCJA doubled the maximum allowance to $1 million, beginning in 2018. This Section 179 allowance is indexed for inflation. The figure for 2020 is $1.04 million.

For instance, if you spend $100,000 on qualified items and they're used strictly for business, you can take an immediate $100,000 deduction in 2020. If those items are used 60% for business, you can take a $60,000 deduction. Although the Section 179 deduction is limited to the amount of your business income, any remainder is eligible for "bonus depreciation" and regular depreciation deductions over time. The TCJA doubled 50% bonus depreciation to 100%, subject to a gradual reduction of the percentage after five years. *Note:* Other special rules may apply to deductions for home computers.

Deduct medical expenses without qualifying for exemption

The TCJA eliminates personal exemptions,

including those claimed for qualifying children and relatives for 2018 through 2025. But just because you aren't eligible to claim a dependency exemption for a parent or other relative doesn't mean that you must lose out on deducting medical expenses you've paid.

For example, suppose Jane provides more than half of her father's total support in 2020. In this case, Jane can still include payments for medical expenses on his behalf among her own medical expenses on her 2020 tax return.

The TCJA enhanced the medical expense deduction. Previously, qualified expenses were deductible above a threshold of 10% of AGI. The threshold was lowered to 7.5% of AGI, but for 2017 and 2018 only. The medical expense deduction threshold was scheduled to revert back to 10% of AGI for 2019 and thereafter, but the 2019 spending law has extended the lower 7.5%-of-AGI threshold through 2020.

Break out medical expenses for tuition

Even if you qualify for a higher education tax credit, it's still a drop in the bucket when you're paying to send a child to college. Plus, these tax breaks are phased out for upper-income taxpayers. But there still may be a way you can squeeze some tax benefits out of tuition payments for a child.

Strategy: Obtain a breakdown from the college on how the tuition is being spent. Make sure you get a statement in writing.

If the school allocates a portion of the cost to health insurance services, you can treat that amount as a deductible medical expense if the student would have qualified as your tax dependent.

Under the current tax rules, however, you can only deduct medical expenses in excess of 7.5% of adjusted gross income (AGI). Under the TCJA, the threshold was lowered from 10% for 2017 and 2018 and the lower threshold has now been extended through 2020.

Caveat: Note that the portion of the tuition payment is deductible as a medical expense only if the school provides the breakdown or it is "readily ascertainable."

Furthermore, if a child attends a special school for a learning disability or other disability—for example, if the child is hearing-impaired and requires special instruction—the parents can treat the entire tuition cost as a medical expense.

Take home-office deductions

Some people have shied away when they could claim a home-office deduction. For many years, this was especially true for taxpayers with more than one business location or no clear-cut business office.

However, starting in 1999, the rule for home-office deductions became much simpler. As long as the taxpayer uses the office regularly and exclusively for necessary administrative or management activities (such as billing) and doesn't regularly use another fixed location for these functions, he will qualify for deductions. A taxpayer also qualifies if he regularly uses the space to meet with clients and customers or if the office is in a structure separate from the residence. Remember, in all cases he must use the office strictly for business reasons during the entire year.

Note that the TCJA eliminates the miscellaneous expense deduction for 2018 through 2025. Therefore, employees who previously claimed deductions for unreimbursed business expenses, like certain home office expenses of employees, currently get no tax benefit.

Turn nondeductible allowance into deductible wages

Many parents pay their kids an allowance without any real strings attached. Instead, they could take a deduction by paying them to do some business-related work, such as cleaning, filing, photocopying or making trips to the post office.

For instance, suppose Ed is self-employed and pays his 15-year-old son $50 per week as compensation for doing odd jobs. The compensation is fully deductible. Depending on Ed's tax bracket, that could save about $700 per year. Plus, it's good for kids to learn what it's like to work for their money.

Is there a trap? Not as long as the work performed and the compensation are reasonable. But it's important to keep records to prove the children worked for the business and weren't overpaid.

Create a triple tax break: Hire your children

Parents have at least three tax incentives for hiring their children to help them in a business or profession:

- **Tax Break No. 1.** Suppose Joe is in a 40% tax bracket, including federal, state and local income taxes. He pays $3,200 to his teenager and deducts the expense. Thus, Joe saves $1,280 on income taxes, while his teenager (assuming no other income) owes no income taxes. (The child's income is sheltered by his or her standard deduction ($12,400 for single filers in 2020).

- **Tax Break No. 2.** As an employee, the teenager is eligible for the same tax-free fringe benefits as other companies are. For example, he or she may participate in a 401(k) plan or take advantage of an educational assistance plan.

- **Tax Break No. 3.** If the business is a sole proprietorship, single-member LLC or husband-wife partnership and the child is under age 18, the taxpayer is excused from paying Social Security, Medicare and federal unemployment taxes.

How to keep a business 'all in the family'

Many closely held companies conform to this profile: An individual founded the business, has run it for years, is ready to retire and plans to transfer it to a son or daughter. So he or she must transfer ownership of the company to the next generation.

The more successful the business becomes, the greater the tax cost of this transfer because income, estate and gift taxes are progressive. So a company often runs into a tax disaster:

- **The transfer isn't done** because the founder never consults a tax adviser.

- **The founder has a tax adviser** but procrastinates, so the transfer isn't made.

- **The transfer is made** but handled badly, and the founder's family pays high taxes.

To avoid all these scenarios, formulate a transfer plan. One of the best ways to implement your plan is to sell some of your stock to the family member who will likely be taking over the business, coupled with a redemption in which the corporation buys the rest of the stock. Thus, your successor will own the outstanding stock and control the business.

Generally, you, the owner, will owe tax on the difference between the sales and redemption proceeds and the basis in the stock, but the gain qualifies for the 15% rate on long-term capital gains (20% for certain high-income taxpayers).

Another way to keep ownership of a business in the family, while minimizing gift and estate taxes to boot, is with a family limited partnership. (*See Chapter 5.*)

Yet another technique for reducing gift and estate taxes: Commission a study showing the company's future cash requirements for R&D and capital equipment to stay competitive or a study showing the industry's future. If the studies show that future cash requirements will be high or that industry prospects aren't bright, this will establish a lower value for the ownership interest for gift tax purposes.

Tax-free cars for the whole family

The cost of operating and maintaining a car used for business purposes, including depreciation, is deductible. If you own a business, the firm can provide cars for the entire family. As long as they're employees who use the cars exclusively for business purposes, the company can deduct the entire cost of operating them. Deductible car expenses include the cost of gasoline, oil, repairs, insurance, depreciation, interest on loans used to purchase the car, taxes, licenses, garage rents, parking fees and tolls.

If you or a family member uses the car for both personal and business use, the value of the personal use is taxed to the user (unless the personal use is negligible).

You can deduct auto expenses using a standard mileage rate, which the IRS sets each year. The rate for 2020 is 57.5 cents per mile, plus business-related tolls and parking fees.

Use of the standard mileage allowance is limited to individuals using passenger cars (including pickups or vans) who:

- **Own the car.**

- **Don't use the car** for hire.

- **Don't use more than** four cars for business simultaneously.

- **Haven't claimed** accelerated depreciation on the car in a prior year.

- **Haven't claimed** Section 179 first-year depreciation on the car.

If you use more than one car for business on an alternating basis, the standard mileage rate is available if both cars otherwise qualify. For example, if Heather uses her spouse's car while hers is in the shop, she can add the mileage and use the standard rate.

To use the standard mileage rate, taxpayers must maintain adequate records to show how many business miles they drove. Estimates won't satisfy the IRS. Remember to keep a log and make entries every day to show where you drove on business and how many miles you put on the car.

Big deductions for 'heavy-duty' SUVs

Here's a little tax secret you may be surprised to learn: You probably can immediately deduct a bigger-than-usual percentage of the cost of buying a sport utility vehicle (SUV), pickup or van if it weighs over a certain amount. This is an exception to the depreciation rules that generally apply to passenger cars, light trucks and lighter SUVs used for business purposes. In fact, depending on your circumstances, you may be able to deduct the entire cost of a heavy-duty SUV under the TCJA, even one that costs $50,000 or up!

For starters, the American Jobs Creation Act of 2004 imposed a reduced $25,000 limit on Section 179 deductions for heavy-duty SUVs placed in service after Oct. 22, 2004. That created a tax advantage when compared to a similarly priced car, light truck or van. This is especially beneficial due to the 100% "bonus depreciation."

Example: Ben buys a qualified heavy vehicle in 2020 for $50,000 and uses it 80% for business. That means its tax basis is $40,000 (80% of $50,000). Under the TCJA, Ben is eligible to claim both the Section 179 deduction and 100% bonus depreciation for 2020. As a result, he can deduct 50% of the $50,000 coast, or $40,000, in the first year of ownership before he even starts taking regular depreciation deductions on the $10,000 remainder. And if Ben uses the heavy-duty SUV 100% for business, he can deduct the entire $50,000 cost in 2020.

Note: The bonus depreciation tax break was increased to 100% for qualified property placed in service from Sept. 9, 2010, through Dec. 31, 2011. It was generally reduced to 50% for qualified property placed in service in 2012 and subsequent legislation eventually extended the 50% deduction through 2017. Now the TCJA resurrects 100% bonus depreciation for five years, beginning in 2018, before gradually phasing it out over the following five years.

Keep good records of charitable gifts

If you give cash to a qualified charity, you can deduct donations within generous tax law limits. But the Pension Protection Act of 2006 (PPA) tightened the rules for substantiating charitable donations of cash or cash equivalents.

Currently, deductions aren't allowed for any contribution of cash, check or other monetary gift *unless* you can show a bank record or written communication from the charity indicating the charity's name, the amount of your contribution and the date you made the donation.

To ensure bulletproof deductions, write checks to charity. Alternatively, you can charge the donation on a credit card or debit card, which you can substantiate with your bank statement. Another PPA change denies deductions for clothing and household goods unless they're in good condition.

Find loophole for home equity debt

Under prior law, you could generally deduct all the "qualified residence interest" (commonly called "mortgage interest") paid during the year. To qualify for the deduction, you must be legally obligated to pay the mortgage, and it must be secured by a qualified home. The home may be your principal residence or one other home like a vacation home.

The deduction limit depends on whether the debt is an acquisition debt or a home equity debt.

- **Acquisition debt:** This is a debt incurred to buy, build or substantially improve a qualified home. Prior to the TCJA, mortgage interest paid on up to $1 million of acquisition debt was fully deductible.

- **Home equity debt:** Any other qualified debt, such as a home equity loan or line of credit, is treated as home equity debt. The mortgage interest paid on up to $100,000 of home equity debt was deductible regardless of how the proceeds were used.

But now the TCJA changes the tax landscape. For acquisition debt, the threshold is lowered from $1 million to $750,000 for 2018 through 2025. The new limit generally applies to debts incurred after December 15, 2017. (However, deductions for existing acquisition debts are grandfathered even if they are subsequently refinanced up to the remaining amount of debt.)

Even worse, the deduction for interest on home equity debt is completely eliminated after 2017 and is suspended through 2025.

Tax loophole: If you take out a new home equity loan or line of credit and use the proceeds for home improvements—say, a fished basement or a new deck—the debt is treated as acquisition debt, rather than home equity debt. Reason: It is a debt incurred to "substantially improve" a qualified residence. Thus, the interest can be deducted going forward as long as you stay below the new $750,000 threshold for acquisition debt.

In fact, just a small change in the way you handle your money can salvage a deduction. For instance, if you were planning to use funds stashed in a bank account for a home improvement and take out a home equity loan to help pay for some of your child's college expenses, you might do the exact opposite. This converts a nondeductible interest expense into a deductible one.

3. Strategies for Business Owners

Only a few of the great family fortunes in the United States were started by passive investors. The Fords, Mellons and Rockefellers all amassed wealth because they understood that owning a business is one of the best means to keep money in the family.

Today's business owners can keep similar tabs on their wealth. The current tax code favors entrepreneurs. Washington encourages the entrepreneurial spirit because new businesses create jobs and stimulate the economy. In return, Congress offers the business owner many tax-saving opportunities.

Unfortunately, it's not that simple. The tax code changes so rapidly that business owners, focusing on their own companies, may not want to devote the time or the resources to keep up with the rules. Furthermore, improperly informed business owners may miss out on available tax-saving opportunities. If you run your own business or are planning a start-up, you'll find many opportunities in this chapter to increase deductions, reduce tax liability and amass more wealth.

Choosing best form of business organization

No matter what type of business, the form of business organization that you use will have a significant impact on your net worth. Here are some key points about the four major forms of organization:

Sole Proprietorship. A sole owner controls the business and takes all the profits, which are included in personal income. Any losses can be deducted from the owner's personal income. No legal formalities are required, and it's easy to start up or close down the business. However, the owner is responsible for all business debts, so personal assets are at risk. In turn, that risk may limit the ability to raise capital, so expansion may be difficult. Similarly, the owner may not be able to attract key employees who want an ownership stake.

Partnership. With two or more owners, more people can invest in the business and share in the profits or use losses to offset other income. Partners are taxed like sole proprietors; except for passive limited partners, each partner is liable for the partnership's debts. Consequently, partners need to work well together.

If one partner dies or leaves the business, the other partners may then have to buy out his share or find a new partner.

Corporation. Most larger businesses incorporate. Then the corporation, not the owners, bears the liability for actions taken by the business.

The state must approve the incorporation, and shares of stock must be issued. If a stockholder dies, the corporation remains intact. Because a corporation can sell more stock to raise capital, it has greater growth potential than other types of business organization.

Regular C corporations are subject to a corporate income tax, but the TCJA has lowered rates beginning in 2018. It replaced the graduated rate structure, featuring a top rate of 35%, with a flat rate of 21%. Qualified dividends paid to employee-shareholders are taxed as personal income, but the maximum rate is 15% (20% for certain high-income taxpayers). However, many small businesses can qualify as "S corporations," thus eliminating the corporate income tax. S corporation shareholders enjoy some of the tax benefits of partnerships: They may currently deduct business losses or carry them forward to future years. In addition, as with other pass-through entities like partnerships, S corporations may qualify for a new 20% deduction under the TCJA.

Limited Liability Company (LLC). Like corporations, LLCs must be set up under state law. LLC owners, referred to as members, are generally shielded from the LLC's debts and liabilities unless they expressly guarantee or assume them (again, this is similar to the corporate situation).

The big difference between LLCs and corporations: Multimember LLCs are generally taxed under the favorable federal income tax rules for partnerships. Single-member LLCs owned by one individual (allowed in all but a few states) can be treated as if they don't exist for federal tax purposes; in other words, the tax rules for sole proprietorships generally apply.

LLCs are attractive because they combine the corporate limited liability advantage with favorable (and more flexible) tax rules applying to partnerships and sole proprietorships. They may also benefit from the new 20% pass-through entity deduction.

Build wealth by not incorporating

You can organize your business as a sole proprietorship, a partnership, an LLC or a corporation. From a tax point of view, incorporating as a C corporation has a significant disadvantage. There's a corporate income tax to pay on top of any personal income taxes due.

If an owner expects to liquidate or sell the corporation, after-tax earnings left in it will be subject to additional tax. Similarly, if after-tax earnings are to be distributed as dividends, recipients will owe income tax and the corporation will receive no deduction. Therefore, you may be able to reduce your total tax bill and build wealth by operating the business as a sole proprietorship, a partnership, an LLC or an S corporation. (*See below.*)

However, the tax advantages of pass-through entities have been reduced somewhat due to the lower tax rate for C corporations, beginning in 2018. In fact, with individual tax rates as high as 37% for owners of pass-through entities, some business owners may opt for the C corporation setup, especially if they don't qualify for the maximum 20% deduction for pass-through entities. This requires an in-depth analysis of your personal situation.

Cut taxes with S corporation

It's possible to shrink two taxes into one by electing S corporation status for a company. An S corporation avoids the corporate income tax, so the owner pays taxes only once, on personal income. If desired, the owner can give shares of the S corporation stock to children or other relatives. Generally, the income will be taxed at their lower tax rates although it may trigger "kiddie tax" complications (*see page 49*).

Giving away shares also reduces your estate tax obligation. If you retain most of the voting shares, however, you can maintain control over the company.

To qualify for an S corporation election, a company must meet several conditions:

* **Be a domestic** company.

* **Have no more than 100** stockholders.

* **Have as stockholders** only individuals or estates. (Some trusts and tax-exempt entities also qualify.)

* **Not have nonresident** aliens as shareholders.

* **Have only one class of stock.**

* **Make the proper election.**

Use S corporation to cut FICA taxes

Self-employed business people quickly find out that the federal self-employment (SE) tax can be just as burdensome as the income tax. The SE tax is the self-employed's version of the FICA tax withheld from the wages of employees. Both are used to fund Social Security and Medicare, so we'll refer to both as Social Security taxes for simplicity.

You may want to consider operating your business as an S corporation to save Social Security taxes. Here's the deal:

The taxable income and deductions of an S corporation are passed through to the owners and included on their Form 1040s. Passed-through income isn't subject to either the FICA or SE tax.

Normally, wages paid to the owner are subject to a combined 15.3% FICA tax: The S corporation is responsible for the employer's share (7.65%), and the shareholder-employee pays the other half (7.65%) on amounts up to the annual "wage base" ($137,700 for 2020). On any amount above the wage base, the S corp and the shareholder-employee each pay 1.45%, for a combined rate of 2.9%.

The usual tax-planning idea is to have the owner receive a relatively low salary (which minimizes FICA tax) and pay out the rest of the corporation's income in the form of S corp distributions. As a result, the owner receives all the cash without the big Social Security tax bite.

Example: Say the taxable income of Carolyn's business (before salary) is $90,000. She draws a salary of $40,000; only that amount is subject to tax. The remaining $50,000 could be distributed to her without any FICA or SE tax. So the FICA tax would be only $3,060 (7.65% x $40,000).

By contrast, if Carolyn ran the same business as a sole proprietorship or single-member LLC, she would pay over twice as much SE tax!

The key point: The $40,000 salary must be reasonable under the circumstances surrounding the business. If it's clearly too low, Carolyn runs the risk of an IRS audit and reclassifying the S corporation distributions as additional salary. If that happens, she will be assessed back FICA taxes as well as possibly interest and penalties.

This idea works best if the business isn't limited to delivery of personal services. In that case, an S corporation owner would have a hard time arguing that all the corporation's income shouldn't be treated as salary.

Collect a new deduction for pass-through entities

The TCJA establishes a new deduction for owners of pass-through entities. Pass-through entity owners who qualify can deduct up to 20% of their net business income from their income taxes, thereby effectively reducing their income tax rate by 20%. This deduction takes effect in 2018 and is scheduled to sunset after 2025.

The deduction is available to S corporations, partnerships, limited liability companies (LLCs) and sole proprietors. If you qualify, you may

deduct up to 20% of your "qualified business income" (QBI) from each pass-through business you operate. This is determined by subtracting all your regular business deductions from your total business income. Any loss is carried forward to next year. In addition, the deduction can't exceed 20% of your taxable income.

For example, Fritz earns $100,000 from his consulting business in 2020. He is a single filer with no other income and claims the $12,400 standard deduction. So his taxable income for 2020 is $87,600. Fritz's pass-through deduction can't exceed $17,520 (20% of $87,600).

The pass-through entity deduction is subject to two phase-out rules. The phase-out thresholds for 2020 are between $163,300 and $213,300 of taxable income for single filers and $326,600 and $426,600 of taxable income for joint filers.

1. Service provider limit: If you're in a specified service business—practically every service provider except architects and engineers—your deduction is phased out gradually and you get no deduction if your taxable income exceeds the upper threshold.

2. Wage and capital limit: The deduction can't exceed the greater of:
- 50% of your share W-2 employee wages paid by the business, or
- 25% of W-2 wages plus 2.5% of the acquisition cost of your depreciable business property.

In this case, you may still qualify for a reduced deduction if your taxable income exceeds the upper threshold.

The rules for calculating the deduction phase-outs are extremely complex. Consult with a tax professional for more details.

Increase liquidity, save taxes with buy-sell agreement

Buy-sell agreements are primarily intended to create a ready market for closely held business ownership interests. Without one, it can be difficult or impossible to cash out when an owner retires, dies or simply wants to liquidate his investment.

Some agreements call for the other owners to buy out the withdrawing owner; these are called cross-purchase agreements. Alternatively, the deal may require the corporation, partnership or LLC itself to cash out the withdrawing owner under a so-called redemption or liquidation agreement.

In addition to providing liquidity, buy-sell agreements should be designed to yield the best tax results for the owners. This area is often forgotten by some attorneys, who simply serve up boilerplate language to their clients.

Some important points to keep in mind when drafting or amending buy-sell deals:

C corporation stock. When the business is a C corporation, the buy-sell agreement should generally be structured as a cross-purchase arrangement rather than as a stock redemption. This is mainly because the remaining shareholders receive no step-up in basis for their shares under redemption deals.

With a cross-purchase agreement, the selling shareholder qualifies for the 15% rate on stock sale gains (20% for certain high-income taxpayers) as long as she has owned the shares more than 12 months. On top of that, the other shareholders receive additional basis in their stock that's equal to what they pay to the departing shareholder.

S corporation stock. As you know, S corporations must meet special rules to maintain their S elections. Accordingly, it's a good idea to include special restrictions in S corporation buy-sell agreements to help ensure the corporation will continue to qualify. In addition, other restrictions that take into account unique S corporation tax rules are generally appropriate.

For example, agreements should include language prohibiting shareholders and/or the corporation from taking the following actions, which would terminate the S election:

1. **Transferring** or issuing shares to a corporation, partnership, ineligible trust or nonresident alien individual.

2. **Transferring** or issuing shares to a new shareholder if the result would violate the 100-shareholder rule.

3. **Giving up** U.S. citizenship (or abandoning residence in the United States for resident alien shareholders).

4. **Issuing** a second class of stock (such as preferred stock).

5. **Voluntary** revocation by the corporation of its S status unless all shareholders agree to do so.

The following buy-sell agreement clauses are intended to deal with shareholder tax issues caused by the corporation's S status:

■ **The company should be required** to allocate its taxable income, gains, deductions, losses and credits using the "closing of the books" method when an owner sells his shares. This is the alternative to the per-share-per-day method, which allocates all tax items as if they occurred ratably throughout the year. The per-share-per-day method can cause extremely distorted allocations for selling shareholders.

For example, a large gain may occur in the period after a shareholder has sold her stock. Under the per-share-per-day method, the selling shareholder will nevertheless be allocated part of the gain. The "closing of the books" method results in allocating tax items to the periods of the year when they actually occur, which would mean no gain allocation to a shareholder who sells out before the gain transaction occurs.

■ **The corporation should be required** to distribute dividends to all shareholders equal to an agreed-upon percentage of passed-through net income and gains. This allows the shareholders to receive enough cash to pay their individual income tax bills. Without such a clause, the majority owners can "gang up" on minority owners by preventing the corporation from distributing dividends sufficient to pay the shareholder-level taxes on passed-through S corporation income and gains. This may force minority owners to sell out when they otherwise wouldn't.

Caution: The same per-share distribution amount must apply to all shareholders, so as not to violate the one-class-of-stock rule. In other words, the company can't pay bigger dividends to shareholders in higher tax brackets.

■ **Estate tax implications.** If a big chunk of the estate will be the value of the closely held business interest, two potential problems arise. First, there may be no market for the ownership interest, which might have to be sold just to pay estate taxes. Second, the estate will probably have to tangle with the IRS over valuing the business interest for estate tax purposes. Fortunately, a buy-sell agreement can solve both of these problems.

First and foremost, the agreement ensures the ownership interest can be sold at a fair price. The estate's liquidity problem goes away.

In addition, a properly drafted buy-sell agreement will set the estate tax value of a business ownership interest. In other words, the price the estate sells the interest for will then also be used as the value for calculating estate taxes. Thus, you avoid expensive, time-consuming and distracting battles with the IRS.

Reality check: Generally, you can't set an artificially low value in an attempt to save estate taxes by passing along the business to relatives "at a discount." Make sure any buy-sell agreement complies with Section 2703 of the Internal Revenue Code; that's where the estate tax rules covering buy-sell agreements are buried.

Make tax-wise loans to the business

When it comes to pumping new money into a business, there's often a right way and a wrong way. Here are some tips on getting the biggest tax-saving bang for your bucks.

Regular corporations

If the business operates as a C corporation, arrange a loan instead of a contribution of additional capital. Why? Because you can't withdraw part of your equity investment later without worrying about adverse tax consequences.

Most successful operations will have current or accumulated earnings and profits (E&P). That means dividend treatment will apply to all or part of any funds removed from the corporation in the future. This is a poor tax result because dividends are taxable income to the recipient, and the company receives no deductions. In contrast, if you lend the money to the corporation, you can be repaid with interest with no tax problems. The loan principal payments are tax free, and the interest is tax deductible to the corporation, which puts additional cash in your hands without double taxation.

What if the bank is willing to make a loan directly to you, but not to the corporation? No problem. Simply arrange to make a "back-to-back" loan to the company at the same interest rate. Don't use the borrowed funds to make a capital contribution; in that case, you would be forced to take dividend payments to repay the loan from the bank.

S corps, partnerships and LLCs

If the business is an S corporation, partnership or LLC, you can generally withdraw your equity tax free (up to the basis in the ownership interest). This means there's not the critical distinction between equity and debt, as is the case with C corporations.

However, you may still want to use loans as part of the capital structure. For example, if the business needs money and only one owner has available cash, he can make a loan to the entity without altering the equity ownership percentages.

Example: Jimmy and Howie form a 50/50 real estate development partnership. They each contribute $200,000 to get the deal off the ground. Later, the partnership has the chance to buy a piece of property for the bargain price of $100,000. Howie has plenty of cash, but Jimmy has none and the commercial loan market has dried up. In this scenario, they can preserve the 50/50 equity sharing arrangement by arranging for Howie to loan the partnership the $100,000 needed for the property acquisition. The same basic principle applies to S corporations and LLCs (and C corporations) with several shareholders.

Back-to-back loans for S corps

For loss-deduction purposes, S corporation shareholders are limited to the basis in their stock, plus the amount of any loans made by them directly to the corporation. However, shareholders receive no basis from debt inside the S corporation, even if it's all personally guaranteed. Fortunately, it's relatively easy to sidestep this problem. If the lender demands personal guarantees, simply arrange to have the loans made to the shareholders rather than to the corporation. The shareholders can then make back-to-back loans to the company and get the additional tax basis. Financially, the lender and the shareholders are in exactly the same position as if a corporate loan were guaranteed, but the tax results are much better with a back-to-back loan.

When an S corporation receives shareholder loans, you want to make sure the IRS can't recharacterize the loans as equity. If that happens, you risk having a second class of stock, which will invalidate the S election. The easiest way to avoid potential problems is to meet the so-called straight-debt guidelines issued by the government.

Debt must meet four requirements to qualify for this straight-debt safe harbor:

1. **The debt must be a written** unconditional obligation to pay a sum certain on demand or on a specified due date.

2. **The interest rate** and payment dates must not be contingent on profits, the corporation's discretion or similar factors.

3. **The debt can't be directly** or indirectly convertible into stock or any other equity interest in the corporation.

4. **It must be owed** to an individual, estate, trust or tax-exempt entity that's an eligible S corporation shareholder.

Sole proprietorships

If your business is a sole proprietorship, the only real concern is to document carefully which personal loan proceeds went for business expenditures. The interest on those debts qualifies as deductible trade or business interest. Under the TCJA, a qualified can deduct the full amount. Claim the deduction by showing the expense on Schedule C. (Don't use Schedule A for this purpose.)

Lease appreciating assets to the company

Business owners often don't want their C corporations to own assets with high potential for appreciation. Why? The appreciation will probably be hit with double taxation if they sell the assets and try to remove the resulting cash from the company. (Double taxation will also apply if the appreciated assets are distributed to the owner rather than being sold.)

Instead, an owner might keep ownership of the assets and lease it to the company. The lease payments are deductible to the corporation, which is another way to get cash out of the corporation in a tax-efficient manner. The owner reports the lease income and claims the depreciation and interest deductions. If the assets are sold at a big gain, she pays tax only once.

The most obvious candidate for leasing to the company is real estate used in the business, but an owner may be able to use the same arrangement for intangible assets, such as patents and copyrights. Also, remember that owning valuable assets outside the corporation generally means they're not exposed to corporate creditors and business-related liability claims.

If the company has several owners, set up a jointly owned partnership, LLC or S corporation to lease the assets. The above benefits will still be available.

Sell business via tax-free reorganization

Maybe your business is run as a corporation (C or S) and another corporation is willing to buy in through a stock deal. As you know, the general rule is that shareholders must recognize taxable gains when they dispose of their shares. However, the tax code allows shareholders to defer gains in what are termed "tax-free reorganizations."

Under a tax-free reorganization, neither the selling shareholder, the target corporation (e.g., the shareholder's company), nor the corporate buyer recognizes any taxable income. You will receive stock in the acquiring corporation, and those shares will take on the tax basis of the shares in the company you're selling. The seller doesn't recognize the "built-in" capital gain inherent in the old shares until the new shares are sold.

In most cases, a tax-free reorganization will be attractive only if you'll receive publicly traded shares considered to be a decent investment. (If there's a preconceived plan to dump the new shares, it could shoot down the tax-free status of the whole deal.) From the buyer's perspective, there's no step-up in the tax basis of the assets owned by the corporation. However, buyers are often willing to overlook that when they can use their own stock, rather than cash, to make acquisitions.

Although the gory details are beyond the scope of this report, keep in mind that tax-free reorganizations can be legally structured in several ways (e.g., as mergers, straight stock acquisitions, asset acquisitions or using subsidiaries of the acquiring corporation). Selecting the best structure will usually turn on legal issues rather than tax concerns. But different structures require meeting different sets of tax rules to ensure tax-free treatment.

You'll definitely need a skilled tax adviser and a business attorney by your side to pull off a tax-free reorg. The fees you'll pay will be well worth your while when you realize the rewards.

Sell out tax free to ESOP

You may be able to arrange to pull cash out of a C corporation business tax free by selling your shares to an employee stock ownership plan (ESOP). Here's the background.

An ESOP is simply a special type of qualified retirement plan set up for the corporation's employees. However, unlike most other qualified plans, an ESOP is intended to invest primarily in the company's common stock.

The employer (i.e., your company) is allowed to make tax-deductible contributions to the ESOP, and there's no current taxable income to the ESOP participants (the covered employees). A unique advantage of ESOPs: They can borrow money from the corporation, shareholders or third-party lenders. Then the ESOP can use the borrowings as leverage to acquire the initial batch of employer shares from you. A so-called leveraged ESOP offers an impressive package of tax advantages, as described below.

Typically, the corporation will make deductible contributions to the ESOP each year. Over time, the contributions pay off the plan loan principal. They also pay the interest. Eventually, the ESOP owns the corporation. In effect, the corporation makes fully deductible payments covering the ESOP loan interest and principal. The ability to deduct principal payments on a loan used to acquire the stock is a unique tax benefit.

But here's an even better tax break that will benefit you personally: As the owner, you can elect to defer taxable gain on the sale of the shares to the ESOP as long as all sales proceeds are reinvested in qualified replacement securities, which include most publicly traded stocks and bonds.

The deferred gain is built into the replacement securities. They take on a tax basis equal to their price reduced by the deferred gain. The entire transaction amounts to a tax-free rollover into the replacement securities. The deferred gain isn't taxed until the replacement securities are finally sold. At that point, you'll pay a maximum 15% rate on a long-term gain (20% for certain high-income taxpayers).

When all is said and done, you've traded relatively illiquid company stock for high-quality, publicly traded investments and postponed all taxes to boot.

Note that you don't have to roll over all the cash from the sale. But the gain that can be deferred is reduced dollar for dollar by the excess of the proceeds from the ESOP sale over the cost of the replacement securities.

Requirements for tax-free rollover

To qualify for such tax-free rollover treatment, both you, as owner, and the ESOP must meet certain requirements:

- **The company must be** a domestic corporation and have no outstanding publicly traded securities.

- **The owner must invest** in qualified replacement securities during a period beginning three months before and ending 12 months after selling the shares to the ESOP.

- **Immediately after the sale,** the ESOP must own at least 30% of each class of the company's common stock or at least 30% of the total value of all the common stock.

- **The stock that's sold to the ESOP** must be either common stock or convertible preferred.

- **The owner must have held** the stock for at least three years.

- **The owner must make the gain** rollover election with his income tax return for the year of sale to the ESOP and file the return by the due date (with extensions).

- **The ESOP can't allocate** benefits to employees who sell stock tax free to the ESOP or to 25% shareholders who are also employees.

Example: John wants to sell the stock of his C corporation business. The FMV of the company's equity is $5 million. John has owned the stock for years, and the basis is only $200,000. The corporation sets up a leveraged ESOP to buy his shares. The consequences:

1. **The newly formed ESOP** will borrow money from the bank (with a guarantee from the company) to buy John's shares for $5 million in cash.

2. **If John spends the $5 million** to purchase qualified replacement securities (he intends to buy a "market basket" of publicly traded issues), he can defer his entire capital gain of $4.8 million. John's basis in the replacement securities will be $200,000. As he

sells replacement securities, he will recognize long-term capital gains and pay only the 15% or 20% tax.

3. **Over the years,** the corporation will make deductible cash contributions to the ESOP to pay the loan principal and interest. As principal is paid down, the ESOP accounts of the employees will be allocated the resulting "equity" (difference between FMV of the shares and the loan balance). Eventually, the employees own the company free and clear through their ESOP accounts.

Tax-free education for entire family

ATRA permanently extended the tax break allowing up to $5,250 of tax-free employer-paid educational assistance.

But this tax break often isn't available to closely held businesses. That's because "nondiscrimination" rules disallow the benefit for most owner-employees and relatives. Fortunately, there's another way to get tax-free educational dollars into employees' hands and benefit owner-employees.

An employer can deduct "working-condition fringe benefits" and they're not taxable income to the recipient employee. The benefits include employer-paid educational expenses for courses or training that's job related. No nondiscrimination rules apply, so this benefit can be provided to employee-owners and relatives who are employees. A written plan isn't required. Just have the company pay qualifying expenses directly or have the employee turn in the expenses for reimbursement.

Limitations do apply, however. The training must help the employee:

- **Maintain or improve skills** needed in the employee's work.

- **Meet specific employer requirements** or legal or regulatory rules that are a condition of retaining the job classification or the pay rate.

Working-condition-fringe status doesn't apply to education needed to meet established minimum job requirements, such as finishing a degree to qualify for a better position or as a condition of keeping a promotion. Ditto for courses that are part of a program qualifying the employee for a different career, such as a clerk working on a computer science degree. (The IRS takes the position that any time someone earns an undergraduate degree, she automatically becomes qualified for a different career.)

Example: As president and owner of her corporation, Elizabeth takes courses and seminars on computers, marketing and management. The company pays for these, and they qualify as working-condition fringes because Elizabeth's job requires broad skills. Even an M.B.A. degree would be OK in this case. However, if her son is a salesperson and the company pays for him to attend law school at night, that's not a working-condition fringe. The education qualifies him for a new career.

If training doesn't cut it as a working-condition fringe, generally it's still deductible by the employer. But it's taxable compensation to the employee and subject to payroll taxes. That's not horrible, but you should secure working-condition-fringe treatment whenever possible, especially if the benefits go to your entire family.

Big deductions for certain business donations

Generally, business entities can deduct only the depreciated cost basis of tangible business property donated to charity. However, prior to 2012, an enhanced deduction was allowed for qualified gifts of books, computers and food inventory. Generally, the deduction was equal to the property's basis plus one-half the unrealized appreciation (but not more than twice the basis). The deduction could not exceed 10% of the taxable income for the year.

ATRA extended the enhanced deduction for donations of food inventory through 2013, and TIPA extended it for 2014. But the enhanced deductions for gifts of books and computer property were not renewed by ATRA or TIPA. Finally, the PATH Act extended the enhanced deduction for food inventory retroac-

tive to 2016 and made it permanent. This deduction is available only to business entities other than C corporations, while the previous deductions for computers and books had been restricted to C corporations.

Savor extra helpings of tax break for employee meals

The tax law serves up a delicious tax loophole that few companies know about. If the company qualifies, it can deduct costs of on-premises meals for all employees who receive them, including the high-paid group of employee-owners and managers. Frequently, such meals are provided in a company cafeteria or similar eating facility.

However, this tax break has been watered down by the TCJA. Previously, a company could deduct 100% of the qualified costs, as opposed to the usual 50% limit on business meals. The deduction is reduced to 50% for 2018 through 2025. After 2025, no deduction will be allowed.

The basic qualification rule: More than 50% of the employees must receive this benefit for the employer's convenience. If the company passes that test, the on-premises meals are considered a *de minimis* fringe benefit for all employees who receive them. Thus, the employees owe zero tax on the value of the meals they received. This remains true even after the TCJA reduction for the employer's deduction.

Usually, workers will satisfy the convenience-of-the-employer test if they can't leave the business premises for meal breaks because of business reasons. IRS regulations list three sets of circumstances that satisfy the convenience-of-the-employer test:

1. **Meals are provided on premises** so that employees are available for emergency calls that might occur during the meal period. Emergency calls must occur or be reasonably expected to occur to qualify under this standard.

2. **The allowed meal period is short** (only 45 minutes or less) because of the nature

of the business. An example is a company with peak hours during 11:30 a.m. to 1 p.m.

3. **Employees can't otherwise obtain meals** during a reasonable meal period: for example, if there aren't any eating facilities near the office or heavy traffic prevents employees from leaving and returning within their lunch hour.

The first circumstance listed above applies to only a few businesses, such as ambulance companies. The other two could easily apply to your own firm. If on-premises meals are provided to more than 50% of the employees for any of the above three reasons, you're in the clear to start giving free meals to high-salaried employee-owners and managers. The company can deduct 50% of the cost, and none of the employees who receive the benefit will pay tax on its value.

Tap into major tax savings from first-year depreciation break

Over the past few years, Congress has enacted extremely favorable rules that expand first-year depreciation write-offs for small businesses. Due to recent legislation, the main benefits have been preserved. Under the TCJA, the benefits are improved even further, leading to unprecedented tax breaks for acquiring qualified business property.

■ **Higher Section 179 depreciation write-offs.** For most small businesses, one of the best tax law changes in recent years is the preservation and enhancement of the Section 179 first-year depreciation allowance. Thanks to this tax code provision, a business may be able to immediately deduct 100% of the cost of qualified new and used business personal property.

The maximum Section 179 was gradually increased from $25,000 to $250,000 for 2009. The Small Business Jobs Act of 2010 doubled this amount to $500,000 for 2010. Under ATRA and TIPA, the maximum $500,000 deduction was preserved through 2014. Although it was scheduled to drop to $25,000 in 2015, the PATH Act restored the maximum $500,000 deduction retroactive to 2015 and made it permanent, subject to inflation indexing in 2016 and thereafter. Finally, the TCJA permanently doubles the maximum allowance to $1 million for 2018 and thereafter. The inflation-indexed figure for 2020 is $1.04 million.

Bottom line: Those complicated multiyear depreciation schedules may become a distant memory. Frequently, many small business owners will be able to simply write off the entire cost of all business equipment in Year One.

Advisory 1: The Section 179 deduction can't exceed the aggregate business income before the deduction. This limitation prevents one from using the Section 179 break to generate an overall tax loss for the year. This is more likely to create a problem when the Section 179 allowance is relatively modest. *The good news:* A self-employed individual (sole proprietor, LLC member or partner) can count wages, including a spouse's if the couple files jointly, as business income for this purpose.

Advisory 2: The Section 179 allowance is phased out dollar-for-dollar to the extent otherwise qualifying assets costing more than a "specified threshold" are placed in service during the year. This threshold was gradually increased from $200,000 in conjunction with the increases for the maximum deduction. It was $2 million in 2010 and 2011. ATRA preserved the $2 million threshold through 2013. Then TIPA extended it for 2014. Although it was scheduled to drop to $200,000 in 2016, the PATH Act restored the $2 million threshold retroactive to 2015, making it permanent and subject to inflation indexing in 2016 and thereafter. Now the TCJA has increased the threshold to $2.5 million with inflation indexing. The threshold for 2020 is $2.59 million. In the event business property placed in service during 2020 exceeds the $2.59 million threshold, the deduction is reduced on a dollar-for-dollar basis.

■ **Immediate deduction for software costs.** The 2003 Tax Act also made most computer software eligible for the Section 179 allowance, which means a business can deduct the entire cost in Year One. Previously, most software had to be depreciated over 36 months. After several previous extensions, the Section 179 deduction for computer software was extended again through 2013 by ATRA and through 2014 by TIPA. Then the PATH Act restored this tax break retroactive to 2015 and made it permanent.

Bigger tax benefits for bonus depreciation

In addition to the enhanced Section 179 deduction, prior to 2015 a business could previously claim "bonus depreciation" for qualified assets placed in service during the year. This tax break applied to:

* Property with a cost recovery period of 20 years or less.

* Depreciable software that is not amortized over 15 years.

* Qualified leasehold improvements

* Water utility property.

In recent years, the Small Business Jobs Act of 2010 retained 50% bonus depreciation for qualified assets placed in service from Jan. 1, 2010, through Dec. 31, 2010 (through Dec. 31, 2011, for property with a recovery period of 10 years and longer and certain aircraft and transportation property).

Then the 2010 Tax Relief Act generally allowed 100% bonus depreciation deduction for qualified assets placed in service from Sept. 9, 2010, through Dec. 31, 2011. It also allowed 50% bonus depreciation for qualified assets placed in service from Jan. 1, 2012, through Dec. 31, 2012. ATRA extended 50% bonus depreciation through Dec. 31, 2013. TIPA extended this tax break through Dec. 31, 2014. Next, the PATH Act restored 50% bonus depreciation retroactive to 2015 and through 2017 with a scheduled phase-out of 40% for 2018 and 30% for 2019 before completely phasing out.

Finally, under the TCJA, bonus depreciation is bigger and better than ever. Not only does the TCJA undo the phase-out scheduled by the PATH Act, it improves the bonus depreciation deduction and extends it longer.

Among other changes, the TCJA increases the deduction to 100% of qualified business property for property placed in service after September 27, 2017 and through 2022. In the following five years, the deduction is phased out as follows:

* 80% for property placed in service in 2023.

* 60% for property placed in service in 2024.

* 40% for property placed in service in 2025.

* 20% for property placed in service in 2026.

After 2026, the phase-out is complete.

In addition, the TCJA expands the definition of qualified property to include used property and coordinates these changes with other tax code provisions. Bottom line: With the 1-2 punch of Section 179 and bonus depreciation, many small business owners can deduct the full cost of property placed in service over the next few years.

Claim new deduction for family leave wages

The TCJA authorizes a new up-to-25% credit for employers who provide family and medical leave wages to employees.

Briefly stated, the credit is available to employers who provide wages to qualified employees on leave under the Family and Medical Leave Act (FMLA). To receive the credit, employers must provide at least two weeks of leave and compensate workers at a minimum of 50% of their regular earnings.

The credit ranges from 12.5% to 25% of the cost of each hour of paid leave, depending on how much of a worker's regular earnings the benefit replaces. The IRS issued additional guidance in 2018 on this new tax break. Consult with a tax professional for more details.

The spending law extends this deduction through 2020.

Take the sting out of the AMT

For years, Congress put Band-Aids on the growing problem known as the "alternative minimum tax" (AMT). But those changes often came too little, too late for individual taxpayers bearing the brunt of the AMT sting.

The AMT, which uses a structure of only two tax rates of 26% and 28%, requires a complex calculation involving exemption amounts. In 2001, Congress bumped up the AMT exemption amounts but only for 2001 to 2004. After it extended meager tax relief through 2005, the Tax Increase Prevention and Reconciliation Act (TIPRA) preserved slightly higher exemption amounts for 2006. Congress passed some late tax relief for tax filers in 2007 and 2008. The American Recovery and Reinvestment Act included another "patch" for 2009. Then the 2010 Tax Relief Act patched the AMT again for 2010 and 2011.

ATRA provided some permanent AMT relief by increasing the exemption amounts, retroactive to the 2012 tax year, and authorizing indexing for inflation the exemption amounts and phaseout thresholds in future years. It also allowed nonrefundable personal credits to offset the full amount of an individual's regular tax and AMT liability. But note that the applicable AMT exemption continues to be reduced when AMT income exceeds certain thresholds.

The TCJA finally delivers more substantial tax relief. Beginning in 2018, it substantially increases the exemption amounts and threshold for phasing out exemptions. The figures for 2020 are as follows:

- The exemption amount for single filers is $72,900 and $113,400 for joint filers.

- The threshold for phasing out exemptions for single filers begins at $518,400 and $1,036,800 for joint filers.

As a result of these changes, many tax filers who had to pay the AMT in the past won't be liable for the AMT any longer.

In any event, if you may still be liable for the AMT, here are four ways you may be able to cut it down to size:

1. **Put some ISOs on hold.** You may own incentive stock options (ISOs) that permit you to buy company stock at a stated exercise price. You can exercise the options tax free as well as qualifying for low-taxed capital gain when the stock is sold. But the bargain element of the ISO (the difference between the option price and fair market value at the time it's exercised) is considered a "tax preference" item for AMT purposes.

    Advice: Figure out with your tax adviser how many ISOs you can exercise this year without triggering AMT consequences.

2. **Adjust back on prepayments** of state income taxes and property taxes. These payments are deductible in the regular income tax calculation, up to an annual total of $10,000, but not for the AMT calculation. Thus, those in high-tax states are more vulnerable to the tax.

    Previously, a common tax-planning move was to prepay state and local taxes at year-end to boost deductions on the taxpayer's regular tax bill.

    But there's no benefit from these payments if you're forced to pay the AMT. Check with your tax adviser before making end-of-year prepayments. He or she can tell you how much to prepay before reaching the point where you gain no benefit.

3. **Be wary about investments.** Long-term capital gains and qualified dividends continue to be taxed at a maximum rate of 15% (although the rate increases to 20% for certain high-income taxpayers). But remember that low-taxed gains and dividends still count toward the exemption levels. *Note:* Municipal bonds are exempt from federal income tax, but if you invest in "private activity bonds" (e.g., municipal bonds used to finance an industrial park), the tax-free interest is added back for AMT purposes. (This AMT adjustment was temporarily suspended for 2009 and 2010.) Depending

on your situation, it may be best to opt for other types of municipal bonds that won't cause AMT problems.

4. **Consider leasing equipment.** It's common for unincorporated business owners to trigger AMT problems by claiming accelerated depreciation deductions for business assets. If you fit in this category, you might lease new equipment instead of buying. The deductions claimed for leasing are allowed for both AMT and regular income tax purposes.

Also, remember to monitor the AMT as the year progresses. If you're near the borderline of paying the AMT, you should step away from "tax preference" items. On the other hand, some high-income taxpayers who can't beat the AMT might as well join it. They should consider accelerating some extra taxable income into 2020 if they're sure that they'll have to pay the AMT without generating an AMT credit. That way, any extra income triggered this year will be taxed at a rate no higher than 28%, as opposed to the top regular tax of 37%.

4. Build Tax-Sheltered Wealth in Retirement Plans

Although tax reform has eliminated many tax shelters, Congress left one area virtually unscathed: qualified retirement plans. In fact, EGTRRA greatly expanded the tax benefits; subsequent laws have enhanced those changes. In a qualified plan, all contributions are fully deductible, with slim chance of an IRS challenge. In addition, a participant's account grows tax-free inside the qualifying plan.

When you finally take the money out of your plans and pay taxes, you may be in a lower tax bracket, meaning you pay less in taxes later rather than sooner. Meanwhile, you've been able to enjoy the benefit of tax-free compounding.

A simple way for you to double retirement savings

If you are self-employed or run a small business, a Simplified Employee Pension (SEP) can provide the benefits of a formal plan without the record-keeping and actuarial expense. An SEP is similar to an IRA, but your annual contributions aren't limited to $6,000 (in 2020).

Instead, the maximum deductible contribution for a SEP in 2020 is 25% of compensation or $57,000 per year, whichever is less. (For the self-employed, the limit for a SEP is 20% of self-employment income.)

The contribution not only reduces taxable income but also grows tax deferred until withdrawals are made. This tax-free compounding may double a long-term savings program.

Unlike other types of retirement plans, which require detailed reports to the IRS, a SEP generally requires only that the person fill out IRS Form 5305-SEP when the plan begins. Moreover, SEPs are handy last-minute planning tools. You can open up a SEP as late as the tax return due date for the current year's return and make a "look-back" contribution that's deductible for the previous year.

How to withdraw money from qualified plans

For an IRA (other than a Roth IRA), a Keogh or a corporate qualified retirement plan, whatever goes in must come out someday, along with all the compound earnings. Except for contributions made with nondeductible dollars, all money inside the plan will be taxed upon withdrawal.

It's advisable to delay retirement plan distributions until past age 59½ unless you're desperate for cash. Earlier distributions will generally be hit with a 10% penalty tax, in addition to the applicable income tax. After age 59½, you can dip into your retirement plan as rapidly as you like without a tax penalty. Assuming that you need the income, you may have to choose between a lump sum and periodic payments.

Other types of retirement plans offer tax benefits for lump-sum withdrawals (i.e., for those born before 1936), but IRAs don't. Individuals must pay income tax at their regular rates. Therefore, you should take IRA withdrawals (and pay income tax) gradually, as you need the money.

What tax benefits do other types of retirement plans offer? If a participant has been in the plan for five or more years, was born before 1936 and receives a lump sum at retirement, he or she may be eligible for 10-year averaging, which can substantially reduce the tax bill. Beneficiaries may use this method if the participant qualifies.

In addition to lump sums, employer-sponsored plans may offer a choice of annuities, a monthly payout plan guaranteed to extend for life or (with lower monthly payments) the lifetime of the participant and spouse. In return for bearing the risk of longevity, however, the employer will pay participants a relatively low return on their retirement account if they take an annuity option. So if you're sophisticated in handling money and qualify for 10-year averaging, you should consider taking a lump sum from a retirement plan, if offered. You can pay the tax and then have full use of the funds.

If you don't need your retirement money right away, you're generally better off letting the funds stay where they are and enjoy tax-deferred compounding. That's true for an IRA or Keogh plan, where the individual is in control. For employer-sponsored plans, you can take a lump sum (if that option is available) and roll it over tax-free into an IRA within 60 days. There's no income tax withholding on a trustee-to-trustee transfer.

Even if you have no pressing need for income, the time will come when you must start withdrawing money from retirement plans. However, the SECURE Act changes the rules for these "required minimum distributions" (RMDs) beginning January 1, 2020. Previously, distributions had to begin no later than April 1 of the calendar year following the year in which the participant reached age 70½. (If someone is still working and isn't a 5% owner of the company, he or she can delay the start date for RMDs from the plan until April 1 of the year after retirement.) The SECURE Act pushes the requirement back to age 72.

For example, let's say Jean turns 72 on Feb. 19, 2020. Under the new rules, her distributions must begin by April 1, 2021.

After the initial distribution, Jean must take money out at least once a year, by Dec. 31. In our example, she must take the second distribution by Dec. 31, 2021 (two in one year), then by Dec. 31, 2022, and so forth. The first distribution (April 1, 2021) is based on Jean's account balances at the end of 2019; the Dec. 31, 2021, distribution is based on her balances at the end of 2020.

How much must Jean take out? Enough so that the balance will be paid out over her life expectancy. If someone's life expectancy is 10 years, for example, he or she must withdraw at least 10% of their retirement funds.

If someone is simply taking retirement plan money out of a CD, the bank may calculate the minimum amount required each year. But if an individual's retirement accounts are spread out, the rules are complicated. If too little is taken out, any shortfall is subject to a (nondeductible) 50% penalty tax.

What happens if someone dies while receiving retirement plan distributions? The distributions must continue, payable to the desig- nated beneficiary.

For retirement plans in which no distributions have begun before death, more options are available. Generally, the proceeds must be distributed within five years of death. However, if there's a designated beneficiary, the payments must generally begin by Dec. 31 of the year after death, but they may be extended over the beneficiary's life expectancy, subject to new SECURE Act rules. Generally, effective on January 1, 2020, funds in an inherited account must be paid out within ten years of the owner's death unless an exception applies (i.e., for beneficiaries that are minors, disabled, chronically ill or no more than 10 years younger than the deceased account owner).

In cases where the beneficiary is the spouse, distributions don't have to begin until after the deceased participant would have turned 72. And the income tax obligation doesn't die with the participant. As the beneficiary receives the proceeds, income tax is due on the money received.

The PPA provided greater flexibility to beneficiaries who inherit qualified plan assets. For distributions after 2006, a nonspouse beneficiary can elect to roll over the assets in the decedent's 401(k) account or other qualified plan to his/her own IRA. Prior to the PPA, this benefit was available only to spousal beneficiaries.

SIMPLE retirement plans

Smaller employers (100 or fewer workers) can set up a Savings Incentive Match Plan for Employees (SIMPLE). They aren't subject to the more complicated nondiscrimination rules and benefit limitations that apply to other qualified plans and are available only if the company doesn't sponsor any other qualified plan.

For 2020, employees can elect to contribute up to $13,500 ($16,500 if they are age 50 or older). Matching employer contributions are mandatory and can range from 1% to 3% of employee compensation. Self-employeds also can set up SIMPLE plans, but they're generally not as simple or as effective in saving taxes as the traditional SEP plans. SIMPLE plans involve establishing participant IRA or 401(k) accounts for all employees who earn at least $5,000. Going the IRA route is usually preferable.

If the SIMPLE plan has IRA accounts, the plan can call for both employee and employer contributions. All contributions are 100% vested immediately. Employees can elect to contribute up to $13,500 for 2020 ($16,500 if age 50 or older). Employer contributions are *required*.

Employers have two ways to go here. The employer can match employee elective contributions dollar for dollar up to 3% of employee compensation (with matching contributions as low as 1% permitted in two out of every five years). Or, the employer can simply make contributions equal to 2% of employee compensation for all those earning at least $5,000.

If the SIMPLE plan sets up 401(k) accounts, most of the paperwork burden that's involved in traditional 401(k) plans will apply. In addition, the employer won't have the option of reducing matching contributions to as low as 1% of employee compensation in two out of five years.

Employee contributions to SIMPLE accounts reduce their taxable wages for income tax purposes, but not for Social Security and Medicare tax purposes. Employer contributions aren't subject to payroll taxes, and the company gets a deduction for the taxable year as long as it makes the contribution by the due date (including extensions) of that year's income tax return.

Distributions to employees from SIMPLE accounts are generally treated the same as distributions from IRA accounts. However, a special 25% penalty tax applies to such premature withdrawals from SIMPLE accounts when they occur within two years of the date when the employee starts participating in the plan.

Take advantage of improved IRA rules

For many years, we saw two big problems with IRAs. First, with the relatively skimpy $2,000 limit on annual contributions, IRAs didn't seem worth the trouble. Second, many people simply earned too much to qualify for deductions. But recent tax law changes have corrected these drawbacks. Plus, the PPA preserved higher contribution amounts and other enhancements that were originally scheduled to "sunset" after 2010.

Married couples can make contributions in 2020 of up to $6,000 each even when only one spouse had earnings. The per-person contribution limit increases by $1,000 in 2020 if the IRA owner is 50 or older as of year-end. Note also that you could not previously contribute to a traditional IRA after reaching 70 1/2. Effective January 1, 2020, the SECURE Act removes this age restriction.

Deductible IRAs

For married couples, if both spouses actively participate in a qualified retirement plan (such as a 401(k) at work or a self-employed Keogh or SEP), deductible contributions are phased out. For the 2020 tax year, the phaseout ranges between $104,000 and $124,000 of modified AGI for joint filers and between $65,000 and $75,000 of modified AGI for single filers.

If only one spouse is an active participant, the phaseout range for 2020 is between $196,000 and $206,000 of modified AGI. This means even "upper middle class" couples with a nonworking spouse can deduct $6,000. The "covered" spouse falls under the stricter phaseout rules explained earlier, so higher-income households can't take additional write-offs.

Note: The $6,000 deduction is also available to the "uncovered" spouse if that person works but doesn't participate in an employer-sponsored or self-employed retirement plan. For 2020, the uncovered spouse can contribute an additional $1,000 if age 50 or older as of year-end.

Roth IRAs

For higher-income earners, Roth IRAs offer healthy tax savings. Contributions aren't deductible, but earnings build up tax-free, and you can eventually withdraw your money (including earnings) without owing federal income tax.

The only ground rules: The account must have been open at least five years, and the participant must be 59$\frac{1}{2}$ or older when distributions begin. Taxpayers can also withdraw up to $10,000 tax-free to help finance a first-time home purchase (subject to the five-year rule). And they can always withdraw original non-deductible

Compare Roth to traditional IRA contributions

Even if you have a retirement plan from your business, such as a 401(k), you can supplement your savings with contributions to traditional or Roth IRAs. Depending on your situation, you may contribute to a traditional IRA or a Roth or a combination of the two. *Note:* The ability to contribute to a Roth is phased out for certain high-income taxpayers.

Every situation is different, but Roths often have a tax edge. Unlike a traditional IRA, contributions to a Roth IRA are never tax-deductible, but the Roth offers the lure of tax-free payments. A qualified distribution from a Roth in existence for at least five years (e.g., one made after age 59½) is completely exempt from tax. In addition, under special ordering rules, other payouts may be wholly or partially tax-free.

Conversely, distributions from traditional IRAs are taxable at ordinary income rates up to 37% in 2020, plus a payout could trigger or increase the 3.8% tax on net investment income (NII). Thus, the combined tax rate on traditional IRA distributions may approach or even exceed 50%, counting state and local taxes.

Also, with a traditional IRA, you must begin taking required minimum distributions (RMDs) after age 70½. But the RMD rules don't apply to Roth IRAs during your lifetime. (Heirs must take RMDs over their life expectancies.)

Ask yourself if your top tax rate in retirement will be higher or lower than your current tax rate. This is often the tipping point. Here are five examples that can provide insights.

Example 1: Erica recently started her own business and will be in the 22% bracket in 2020. If the business pans out, she projects to be in the 32% bracket or higher in her retirement years.

Recommendation: Erica should contribute to a Roth this year. While she won't get a deduction, she will avoid paying a higher tax rate on the income and gains that accumulate in the Roth. Plus, she won't have to take RMDs from her Roth.

Example 2: Steven has owned a business for 40 years and is closing in on retirement. At this juncture, he is concerned about the RMDs that must begin in his seventies. In fact, the RMDs may push Steven into a higher tax bracket than he is in now. Assume that he won't need the RMD income to live on.

Recommendation: Steven should contribute to a Roth this year. This way, he won't have to take out additional amounts from his traditional IRAs.

Example 3: Gwen is middle-aged and has owned her business for a couple of decades. During this time, she has been diligent about retirement saving, socking away close to the maximum allowed for 401(k) plans.

Recommendation: Gwen should contribute to a Roth this year. She will have to take RMDs from her 401(k) in her seventies once she stops working, but the Roth IRA contributions can continue to grow untouched.

Example 4: Vance is middle-aged and his business has peaked. But he will qualify for a traditional IRA deduction this year, which he needs for his situation. In addition, based on his calculations, Vance expects to be in a much lower tax bracket in retirement and move to a low-tax or no-tax state.

Recommendation: Vance should contribute to a traditional IRA this year. Not only will he benefit from the current deduction, he will owe low federal income tax when he receives distributions and will pay low or no state income taxes.

(Continued on page 33

(Continued from page 32)

Example 5: Grace is middle-aged and her business is struggling. Based on her calculations, she expects to be in a slightly lower tax bracket in retirement than she is in now.

Recommendation: Grace should contribute to a traditional IRA this year. The contributions may qualify for a current tax deduction that can reduce her tax liability at a time when she is strapped for cash.

Note: Under the TCJA, tax rates are scheduled to return to pre-2018 levels in 2026, but this could change.

---

contributions without any tax or penalty (although this limits the ability to earn additional tax-free income). However, the ability to contribute directly to a Roth IRA is phased out. For single filers in 2020, the phaseout begins at $124,000 of modified AGI and for joint filers it begins at $196,000 of modified AGI.

It may be possible for you to convert a regular IRA into a Roth account. Conversions will be treated as distributions from the regular IRA, a strong consideration for nondeductible accounts. Also, it could make sense for deductible accounts if you are in a low tax bracket and expect to earn many years' worth of tax-free income in the new Roth account. (The 10% penalty tax on distributions before age 59½ doesn't apply to conversions.)

Prior to 2010, conversions to a Roth IRA were allowed only if your AGI was $100,000 or less. For 2011 and thereafter, under TIPRA, you may convert a regular IRA regardless of your income level.

Observation: Roth IRAs may render regular nondeductible IRAs obsolete unless the participant's income is so high that she doesn't qualify to make a Roth contribution. In that case, you can still contribute to regular nondeductible accounts and earn tax-deferred income. However, you'll owe tax on the earnings as you make withdrawals.

Max out tax savings with defined contribution plan

For 2003 and later years, the maximum deductible contribution to a stand-alone defined contribution plan is $40,000, plus an inflation adjustment (up from the 2001 limit of only $25,500), thanks to EGTRRA. As with IRAs, the PPA preserved higher contribution limits for defined contribution plans.

Most small businesses' retirement arrangements, other than 401(k) plans, are set up as standalone defined contribution plans. For example, if Phil's closely held corporation provides a profit-sharing plan or he has a garden-variety Keogh plan for self-employment activity, an inflation-adjusted limit of $57,000 applies to the account in 2020.

In 2003 and subsequent years, the maximum deductible contribution to a standalone defined contribution plan is 25% of compensation or 20% of self-employment income. For this purpose, compensation or self-employment income up to $200,000, plus an inflation adjustment, is considered.

For 2020 the inflation-adjusted limit is $285,000. Thus, both the absolute dollar maximum and the percentage limit are much more generous than they were just a few years ago.

5. Tax-Wise Estate Planning

You may think that you don't have to worry about estate taxes. But it's not automatic for everyone. Upon a person's death, the executor must add up everything the person owns (and the IRS will check the math!). That includes the house, furnishings, other real estate, pension plan, life insurance, investments and collections. Despite the generous breaks afforded by the federal tax law, you still may have some exposure. Plus, you may have state inheritance and death taxes to consider.

It's been a long road to this point. The federal estate tax exemption gradually increased in recent years while the maximum tax rate declined. For example, in 2001, the estate tax exemption was only $675,000 while the maximum tax rate was 55%. But that's when things really started to get interesting.

Under EGTRRA, the estate tax was repealed in 2010, but was reinstated in 2011. The exemption was scheduled to drop to $1 million and the top estate tax rate was scheduled to increase to 55%. Among other changes, the 2010 Tax Relief Act authorized a $5 million exemption (indexed to $5.12 million for 2012) with a top estate tax rate of only 35%. It also repealed the modified carryover basis rules for inherited assets, reunified the estate and gift tax system, and coordinated comparable changes for the generation-skipping tax (GST) affecting most transfers from grandparents.

For a decedent dying in 2010, an executor could elect to use the rules under EGTRRA repealing the estate tax or the 2010 Tax Relief Act rules in effect for 2011.

The progression of the estate tax exemption and the top estate tax rate since 2001 is shown in the following chart.

Year	Estate Tax Exemption	Maximum Rate
2005	1,500,000	47%
2006	2,000,000	46%
2007–2008	2,000,000	45%
2009	3,500,000	45%
2010	Unlimited	Estate tax repeal
2011	5,000,000	35%
2012	5,120,000	35%
2013	5,250,000	40%
2014	5,340,000	40%
2015	5,430,000	40%
2016	5,450,000	40%
2017	5,490,000	40%
2018	11,180,000	40%
2019	11,400,000	40%
2020	11,580,000	40%

However, the estate tax relief afforded by the 2010 Tax Relief Act was only temporary. These provisions were scheduled to "sunset" after 2012.

At long last, ATRA included the following permanent changes, retroactive to Jan. 1, 2012:

- The estate and gift tax system remained unified. Significantly, the estate tax exemption continues to shelter lifetime gifts as well as inheritances.

- The estate tax exemption remained at $5 million (indexed to $5.49 million in 2017).

- The top estate tax rate was bumped up only slightly to 40%.

- Portability of estate tax exemptions between spouses, which had technically expired after 2012, remained in effect.

- Related provisions reflecting the generation-skipping transfer tax (GSTT) were extended.

- The deduction for state estate taxes was

extended. Prior to 2005, a credit against estate taxes was allowed, but it was replaced by the deduction.

Finally, the TCJA doubled the $5 million exemption to $10 million, indexed for inflation. The inflation-indexed exemption for 2020 is $11.58 million.

Despite the slew of recent favorable changes, the federal estate tax burden can still be significant for certain families.

Plus, many states impose taxes on the estate, on heirs or on both. Thus, any tax planning to reduce the taxable estate can mean huge savings for some families.

Live long and prosper from changes to estate tax exemption

EGTRRA contained significant changes on the estate tax front. Until 2010, the federal estate tax continued to exist, as the preceding chart illustrates. Then it was repealed for 2010, only to be revived a year later. As we've said, the estate tax exemption for 2011-2012 was increased to $5 million (indexed to $5.12 million for 2012), with a top estate tax rate of 35%. ATRA established a permanent exemption of $5 million (indexed to $5.49 million in 2017) with a top estate tax rate of 40%. Finally, the TCJA doubled the exemption to $10 million (indexed to $11.58 million in 2020), although it is scheduled to revert to pre-2018 levels after 2025. Therefore, planning to minimize or avoid the federal estate tax continues to be a critical issue for certain high-net-worth individuals, but at least there is greater clarity going into the future.

Other recent tax law changes have an impact on estate planning. For instance, under EGTRRA, heirs inheriting assets in 2010 had to carry over the basis of those assets, instead of receiving a step-up in basis to the value on the date of death. But a surviving spouse could benefit from exceptions totaling up to $4.3 million ($1.3 million for non-spouse beneficiaries). The 2010 Tax Relief Act permanently replaced the carryover basis rules with an unlimited step-up in basis for assets inherited after 2011.

Bottom line: The best estate-planning strategy is to take all these changes into account in developing a comprehensive plan for the future.

'Tis better to give than bequeath

Although the current estate tax exemption is generous, you can reduce your estate during your lifetime by giving gifts.

Each year, an individual is allowed to give away a specified amount without reducing the $10 million lifetime gift tax exemption ($11.58 million in 2020). For 2020, the gift tax exclusion is $15,000 for every recipient. A married couple jointly can give away up to $30,000 per recipient.

Example: Lisa has two children. She and her spouse can give each child $30,000 in 2020 with no tax consequences. If the children are married, they can give each of their spouses (if they wish) up to $30,000 per year. If they have four grandchildren, again they can give each one up to $30,000. In this example, Lisa and her spouse can shrink their taxable estate by $240,000 and use this technique every subsequent year if they choose.

The 2010 Tax Relief Act reunified the estate and gift tax systems for 2011 and 2012. ATRA made that permanent for 2013 and thereafter. Therefore, the lifetime gift tax exclusion is $10 million under the TCJA (indexed to $11.58 million for 2020), while the gift tax rate remains at 40%. Gifts in excess of the annual gift tax exclusion may be sheltered by the lifetime gift tax exclusion, but this effectively reduces the estate tax shelter that will be available to an individual's estate.

The gifts needn't be in cash. You can give away publicly traded securities and put a value on them as of the date of the gift. For other items (real estate, shares in a small business) you should consult with a tax pro on how to set a valuation before making any gifts.

Another gift tax loophole: If a person pays someone else's school tuition or medical bills directly, that money doesn't count. In our example, Lisa can make $15,000/$30,000 annual gifts on top of these direct payments. So in addition to the $240,000, she could reduce her estate even faster with tax-free gifts by, for example, paying for a grandchild's college bills.

Avoid or defer taxes with unlimited marital deduction

Married people can give their spouses as much as they want while alive, with no gift tax obligation (as long as the spouse is a U.S. citizen). At death, there won't be an estate tax obligation for transfers to a spouse. There's no restriction on the amount that can be transferred tax-free under the unlimited marital deduction.

In the past, a spouse may have transferred assets out of his or her name to benefit from the unlimited marital deduction. Another common strategy was to establish a "credit shelter trust" with the maximum amount that may be transferred tax-free (e.g., $11.58 million in 2020) and a separate marital trust for any remaining assets.

Current law allows a spouse's unused estate tax exemption to be portable, so there is less incentive to divide up the transfer of assets to maximize each spouse's estate tax exemption.

Caution: Don't have funds transferred from one spouse's IRA to the other's. That will be treated as a taxable distribution from the transferor's IRA; the result is an immediate income tax bill, plus the 10% penalty tax if this happens before age 59½. Arrange to transfer the ownership of other property to do any asset-balancing.

Use QTIP to keep control

There's a potential problem in using the unlimited marital deduction. Say Marie is the breadwinner and has amassed a $15 million estate. But now she's divorced and has remarried, and her current spouse also has children from a previous marriage.

Marie may not want to give her spouse millions while she's alive because that money probably won't wind up with her children. The same thing may happen if she leaves all her assets to her new spouse in order to use the unlimited marital deduction. Marie's wealth may wind up with her spouse's children, not hers.

In this situation, Marie may decide to use a QTIP (Qualified Terminable Interest Property) trust. Money goes into the trust at death, and the surviving spouse is entitled to all the trust income for as long as he lives. Therefore, the QTIP trust qualifies for the unlimited marital deduction and no estate taxes are due at death.

However, when her spouse dies, the trust assets go to the beneficiaries selected by Marie—her own children, most likely—so she has both tax deferral and control.

Although QTIP trusts are commonly used in second marriages, that's not their only application. Marie could use a QTIP to preserve assets and to protect children in case her surviving spouse remarries after her death. This strategy is also useful if Marie fears that her surviving spouse might squander his inheritance.

Simple tricks of the trade for gifts

For those who may worry that the money they give away will be used unwisely, a so-called Crummey trust is an option. Here, the beneficiary (usually a child or grandchild) has only a limited period following the gift (say 30 days) to withdraw the funds. Once the window of time passes, the money stays in the trust, where you retain control as trustee.

To give away property rather than cash, it's best to unload assets expected to appreciate rapidly. That way, the increase in value will occur outside the estate without risk of a bigger estate tax bite. And if a child or grandchild sells the property, the gain will often be taxed at a lower rate than would apply to the donor.

If you own real estate that has deflated in value, it may now be poised to go up again. It's always darkest before the dawn. You should consider gifting away pieces of property under the annual gift tax exclusion ($15,000 for 2020) to position the kids or grandkids to benefit from future appreciation. However, don't arrange for gifts of mortgaged property with a tax basis less than the debt. That triggers an income tax gain.

Also, it's best to avoid giving depreciated property with a value less than your tax basis.

Instead, sell it, take the loss on your income tax return and then give away the cash.

Don't overlook the fact you can give away any amount to pay for tuition (not room and board or books) at a qualifying educational institution. The same is true for medical expenses. These payments qualify as tax-free gifts above and beyond the annual gift tax exclusion that ordinarily applies, and they don't reduce the $10 million lifetime gift tax exemption (indexed to $11.58 million for 2020). But the donor must make the payment directly to the educational institution or medical care provider.

Finally, you can arrange "deathbed" gifts under the annual gift tax exclusion to reduce your estate in the last few days. How it works: You grant a power of attorney (POA) to a trusted relative or friend (or maybe even your tax adviser) to act on your behalf in financial matters when you're incapacitated. To prevent IRS controversies, it's best for the POA to grant the right specifically to make gifts and to have checks deposited or cashed before death.

Avoid paying estate tax on life insurance coverage

Often, it's life insurance coverage that triggers estate taxes by pushing estates over the prevailing exemption amount. People often overlook this issue because they know life insurance proceeds can be collected without owing any federal income tax. However, no such rule applies for federal estate tax purposes: Proceeds are included in the insured's taxable estate unless she has no "incidents of ownership" in the policy.

In other words, even when life insurance proceeds go directly to a policy beneficiary rather than to the estate, they may still be taxed if, at death, the insured has "incidents of ownership" (e.g., the ability to change beneficiaries, cancel the policy and borrow against the cash value).

There are two basic ways to get life insurance out of an estate. First, you can simply name your spouse as the beneficiary of the policy or provide in your will that your spouse receives the proceeds from the estate. Then, the insurance payout qualifies for the unlimited marital deduction (assuming the spouse is a U.S. citizen). The downside: The funds will eventually end up in your surviving spouse's estate.

If you want to get the proceeds out of both estates, you need to eliminate any incidents of ownership. Solution: Establish an irrevocable life insurance trust to own the policy. This can make sense when removing the insurance brings you down to the magic $10 million level ($11.58 million for 2020). Transfer ownership of the policy to the trust. When the insured dies, the trust receives the insurance money.

The trust should be set up with someone other than your surviving spouse as trustee. The trustee can be directed to make trust fund disbursements to meet your surviving spouse's reasonable financial needs. Upon the death of your surviving spouse, the trust funds can go to beneficiaries named in the trust document (the trust funds aren't included in the estate of the survivor).

If you put a policy with cash value into the trust, you may have a gift that exceeds the annual gift tax exclusion. But the advantages of removing the proceeds from the estate will usually far outweigh that negative. Term insurance policies have no cash value, so they can be transferred without this concern.

You can continue to pay the premiums on the policy, with the payments being treated as gifts. In most cases, the premiums will be below the annual gift tax exclusion, so there's no problem.

Caution: In setting up life insurance trusts, time is of the essence. That's because when a life insurance policy is transferred within three years of death, it will be included in the decedent's estate. Period. That means a transfer to a life insurance trust must be done more than three years before death to achieve the desired results. It's best to act sooner rather than later. Alternatively, to avoid the three-year rule, have the trust purchase new policies on your life and cancel the old ones.

Use second-to-die life insurance to cover estate taxes

Another type of life insurance can help your family handle estate tax. You have to choose between paying now (to an insurance company) and paying much later (to the IRS).

If you're relying on life insurance proceeds to help the kids pay estate tax, whom should they insure? No one knows which parent may die first. Insuring both parents can be an expensive deal.

That's why survivorship life insurance has become so popular over the last few decades. Also called "second-to-die" or "last-to-die" insurance, these policies cover two lives, usually a married couple. There is no payoff after the first death. Upon the second death, the proceeds go to the beneficiaries, typically the children, who can use the money to pay estate tax.

Such policies end the guessing game. No matter which spouse dies first, the life insurance proceeds will be there when they're needed.

There's a price advantage, too. Because the insurance company expects to pay off later, a policy that covers two lives is less expensive, perhaps much less costly, than a policy that covers only one life.

Similarly, the cost of one second-to-die life insurance policy is likely to be less than one single-life policy on each spouse. You pay just one sales commission instead of two; policy administration expenses are halved.

For example, a 62-year-old husband and his wife, age 58, might buy a $1 million second-to-die policy for eight $15,000 premiums: $1 million in coverage for $120,000 in total premiums. As the insurance salespeople like to put it, that's pre-paying estate tax for 12 cents on the dollar.

Recommendation: Shop around before buying a second-to-die policy. Most life insurers offer such policies, and the competition is spirited. You should obtain several price quotes or make sure that your agent does so. The best pick may be a policy that combines low-cost term insurance with permanent insurance, which prevents the term premiums from getting too large over time. Remember, a second-to-die policy provides life insurance coverage, so policies that stress cash-value buildup should be viewed carefully.

Another tip: Don't take every policy illustration at face value. Those illustrations aren't guaranteed; insurance companies are presenting numbers in a way that makes their policies look good.

Finally, be careful about policy ownership. If you or your spouse owns the policy, your children could lose nearly half the value to federal estate tax. However, you may not want your kids to own the policy. Suppose one of them gets divorced in the interim while holding a valuable life insurance policy. To avoid complications, it's advisable to set up an irrevocable life insurance trust to hold the policy. Properly done, that will keep the policy out of your estate.

The perils of joint ownership

Many years ago, brothers Frank and Joe were vacationing in Hawaii. They invested in raw land, each putting up half the money, and declared themselves co-owners. Technically, they were joint tenants with the right of survivorship.

Frank stayed a bachelor, but Joe married, had children and then divorced. Finally, the two brothers decided to sell their Hawaiian property to a Japanese developer, who was offering $2 million. Before the deal was sealed, Joe died.

In his will, Joe left his half of the property to his children. However, because the title was held as "joint tenants with the right of survivorship," his wishes were disregarded. Instead, his share went directly to Frank.

As you can see from this example, joint ownership can be a huge mistake. What are the alternatives? With "fee simple" property, an individual owns the property outright, so he can dispose of it as he wishes. With "tenancy in common," the individual owns property with one or more co-owners, but they can still dispose of their share as wished. However, joint tenants with the right of survivorship must pass their shares to the co-owners when they die.

Joint tenancy (also known as "tenancy by the entirety" in some areas) is simple and convenient and enables property to bypass probate. But joint tenancy has some disadvantages. Since they can't leave their assets to whomever they want, this can cause major estate tax problems.

Suppose, for example, that John and his spouse are joint owners of a house worth $2 million. No matter who dies first, the surviving spouse inherits $1 million worth of house. That may mean assets can't be left to the children, taking advantage of the $11.58 million estate tax exemption for 2020. Then, when the survivor dies and the entire $2 million house passes to the children, they may owe estate taxes.

There are income tax consequences as well. Suppose that the $2 million house was a vacation home purchased for $500,000 many years ago. If John dies first in 2020, his spouse gets a "step-up" in basis on the half that she inherits, to $1 million. But her half of the house still has its $250,000 basis. So if she decides to sell, she'll have a $750,000 taxable gain ($2 million selling price minus $1.25 million in total basis).

Suppose John had owned the entire house. At his death, the wife would inherit the house with a full step-up, to $2 million. She could sell the house for that much and not owe any income taxes.

If joint tenancy can be unfortunate in the case of a first marriage, consider the problems that might occur in a second marriage when each spouse has children from previous marriages. When one spouse dies, the survivor—not the children of the spouse who died—will inherit the decedent's half of the jointly held property.

Even greater problems may arise if the co-owners aren't married. Perhaps a widow and her grown son hold property jointly. Gift tax consequences may loom when they first establish the joint ownership, and all the jointly owned assets must pass to the son at the widow's death, possibly at the expense of her other children.

To avoid such problems, you might prefer fee-simple or tenancy-in-common ownership. As long as those properties are held in a revoca-ble living trust, rather than in your name, they avoid probate.

Reduce estate taxes, but keep control of assets

A limited partnership has general partners and limited partners. Taxable income and losses flow through to the partners with no partnership-level income tax. Typically, the general partners make all the day-to-day decisions; the limited partners have no liability beyond the cash they contribute and notes they personally sign.

Your family can use this structure to trim estate taxes. Let's say Michael Jones starts by creating the "Jones Family Limited Partnership," with 1% or 2% of the interests for general partners. The other 98 or 99% is for the limited partners. At this point, Michael (or he and his spouse) holds all the partnership interests.

The next step is to retitle some of the business or investment assets so that the Jones Family Limited Partnership owns them. Because Michael and his spouse are merely moving assets from one pocket to the other, no gift tax is due.

Now, if Michael wishes, he can give away limited partnership interests to their children and/or grandchildren. Suppose he has $1.5 million worth of assets in the family limited partnership. Each 1% partnership interest will be worth $15,000. So Michael and his spouse could give away 2% per year to their children, their children's spouses and their grandchildren without running into the gift tax. Actually, Michael could probably give away more than 2% per year because the value of any gifted limited-partnership interest should be discounted to reflect that it's a minority ownership interest with restrictions. Over a period of years, he can give away 20%, 50%, up to 98% or 99% of his assets, all held as limited-partnership interests.

What if Michael doesn't want to give away most or nearly all of his assets? That's where the limited partnership structure comes in handy. He (and perhaps his spouse) can hold onto the 1% or 2% general partnership interest and remain in control. The children indirectly own the assets, but they have limited rights. Therefore, a family limited partnership works particularly well for removing real estate or a family business from the estate while still retaining control.

As general partner, Michael decides how much salary he should receive for managing the partnership's assets. Also, he decides how much of the partnership's cash flow to distribute.

Of course, there are trade-offs in return for the estate-planning benefits of the family limited partnership. Michael can't make selective distributions. That is, whatever he gives to the limited partners must be distributed evenly, according to their interests. He can't pay some and not the others.

Michael probably will want to make sure some money is distributed to the limited partners. Under the tax code, all partners must recognize their share of a partnership's taxable income. If that $1.5 million worth of assets in our previous example generates $100,000 worth of taxable income, each 1% interest holder would receive $1,000 worth of taxable income. Each will owe tax on that income, with or without a distribution, so there probably should be some payout.

How to set up a qualified personal residence trust

By setting up a qualified personal residence trust (QPRT), you can get an appreciating home out of your estate and into the hands of your children while continuing to use the property. But you do incur some risks.

Example: Diane wants to give her $450,000 home to her son. Instead of making an outright gift, she makes a gift of the home to the QPRT, which is a form of irrevocable trust with her son named as the beneficiary. Diane should set the trust up with a term that's less than her life expectancy.

The value of a home for gift tax purposes is determined through a complex set of calculations that involve age, current interest rates, the term of the trust and the home's current market value. These calculations might knock the gift tax value of the home down to a mere $200,000. Because the gift has been heavily discounted, the hit to the $11.58 million gift tax exemption for 2020 is minimized. And Diane has successfully removed any future appreciation from her taxable estate.

Diane is allowed to continue living in the home over the term of the trust. After that, ownership passes to her son. Hopefully, she can work out a rental arrangement if she wants to continue living there.

What are the risks?

If Diane dies during the term of the trust, all bets are off and the home's full date-of-death value is included in her estate. On the other hand, if she outlives the trust and wants to stay in the house, she's now at the mercy of the new landlord, her son. Nevertheless, if she can handle these two big uncertainties, a QPRT can be a great estate-planning tool, provided she outlives the term of the trust.

Another tip: If the idea of having an adult child for a landlord makes you queasy about setting up a QPRT for your main residence, consider using the trick for a vacation home instead. If the term of the trust is set up to equal the age at which you will no longer be using the vacation home, that eliminates the biggest negative consideration.

6. Tax-Wise Investing Strategies

You often hear that playing the tax angles shouldn't be the driving force behind investment decisions. To an extent, that's true, but current rules on qualified dividends and long-term capital gains should prompt savvy investors to take a close look at their investment game plan. That's because federal income taxes are usually the biggest item on the expense side of the ledger for investment activities, and recurring legislation has changed many of the rules.

Take advantage of favorable tax rate on dividends

A centerpiece of the 2003 Tax Act was a huge tax rate cut for qualified dividends paid on stock of domestic and qualified foreign corporations held in taxable accounts. These "Bush era" tax cuts were generally preserved by ATRA, although certain high-income individuals are taxed at a higher rate.

Prior to 2003, dividends were taxed as "ordinary income." That meant that dividends could potentially be taxed at the highest individual rate (37% in 2020).

No more. Effective for 2003 through 2012, qualified dividends were essentially taxed the same as long-term capital gains thanks to TIPRA and subsequent legislation, including the 2010 Tax Relief Act. Thus, the maximum rate remained at only 15%.

Even better, individuals in the regular 10% and 15% rate brackets had to pay tax at a rate of only 5% on qualified dividend income (zero percent in 2008 through 2012).

The maximum tax rate of 15% (zero percent for individuals in the regular 10% and 15% tax brackets) was permanently extended by ATRA for 2013 and thereafter. However, a maximum 20% rate was applied to investors in the top ordinary income tax bracket (39.6% in 2017).

Therefore, all but the wealthiest taxpayers can continue to benefit from a rock-bottom tax rate on qualified dividends.

Now the TCJA preserves this preferential tax treatment for qualified dividends with certain modifications. Instead of being tied to tax brackets, the zero percent and 20% tax rates are applied as follows in 2020.

- The zero percent rate applies to single filers with taxable income under $40,000 and under $80,000 for joint filers.

- The 20% rate applies to single filers with taxable income above $441,450 and above $496,600 for joint filers.

Reminder: To be eligible for the reduced rates on qualified dividend income, an investor must hold the stock on which the dividend is paid for more than 60 days during the 120-day period that begins 60 days before the ex-dividend date (the first day shares trade without the right to receive an upcoming dividend payment).

In other words, when investors own shares for only a short time around the ex-dividend date, the dividend is taxed at their regular rate, which can be as high as 37% in 2020.

Caution: The preferential rates don't apply to dividends received in tax-deferred retirement accounts, such as traditional IRAs, 401(k) accounts and SEPs. Dividends accumulated in these accounts will still be taxed at the participant's regular rate when they're withdrawn as cash distributions.

Some dividends don't benefit

The 2003 Tax Act's dividend rate cuts benefit only certain types of dividends. Keep in mind:

- **Some "dividends"** aren't dividends at all. For instance, credit union dividends are really in the nature of interest payments. As such, they're considered ordinary income and therefore taxed at the investor's regular rate.

- **The same is true** for "dividends" paid by certain preferred stock issues that are essentially publicly traded "wrappers" around underlying corporate bonds.

- **Mutual fund dividends** that consist of short-term capital gains, interest income and other types of ordinary income are taxed at regular rates.

- **In contrast, mutual fund dividends** that consist of long-term capital gains and qualified dividends paid on corporate shares owned by the fund are eligible for the favorable rates. Annual mutual fund statements will identify dividend amounts that qualify for the favorable rates as well as those that don't.

- **Many REIT dividends** won't be eligible for the favorable rates. That's because the bulk of REIT payouts are typically not from qualified dividends on stock owned by the REIT or from long-term capital gains. So, most REIT dividends will be ordinary income taxed at regular rates.

- **The favorable rates** on qualified dividends have no impact on investments held in tax-deferred retirement accounts. Dividends accumulated in these accounts are taxed at ordinary rates when withdrawn as cash distributions. You might think then that it would be smarter to hold dividend-paying shares in taxable accounts rather than in tax-advantaged retirement accounts. Not necessarily true.

Updated tax strategies for dividend-paying assets

You should consider holding REIT investments inside tax-advantaged retirement accounts. REIT shares deliver current income (in the form of dividends), plus the potential for capital gains as well as the advantage of diversification. As explained earlier, however, the 2003 Tax Act doesn't treat most REIT shares held in taxable accounts as favorably as garden-variety corporate shares. But REIT shares held in retirement accounts are treated the *same* as the garden-variety shares. So,

other things being equal, retirement accounts now are generally the best place for REIT stocks.

Thanks to recent tax law changes, we no longer see any disadvantage to holding garden-variety corporate shares that pay healthy amounts of qualified dividends in taxable accounts. The favorable rates apply equally to stock returns in the form of qualified dividends and those in the form of long-term capital gains.

Pay only 15% tax rate on long-term capital gains

As you probably know, long-term capital gains from sales *on* or *after* May 6, 2003, are generally taxed at a maximum rate of only 15% (down from 20% before the 2003 Tax Act). Individuals in the 10% and 15% rate brackets had to pay only 5% on long-term gains from sales after the magic date (zero percent in 2008 through 2012). These tax breaks, which were scheduled to expire after 2010, were extended by the 2010 Tax Relief Act.

ATRA permanently extended the maximum 15% tax rate on long-term capital gains (zero percent for individuals in the regular 10% and 15% tax brackets) for 2013 and thereafter. However, as with qualified dividends, ATRA established a maximum 20% tax rate on taxpayers.

Now, as with qualified dividends, these favorable tax rates for long-term capital gains are retained by the TCJA (see first article in this chapter).

Some gains don't qualify for lower rate

For investments held in taxable accounts, it's important to understand that the 2003 tax rate cuts, as extended by subsequent laws, don't benefit certain kinds of capital gains:

- Short-term gains from investments held for one year or less are still taxed as ordinary income, which means regular rates apply. (The maximum rate in 2020 is 37%.) For example, if an investor in the regular 32% tax bracket holds appreciated stock for exactly one year, she could owe the IRS up to 32% of the short-term profit. In contrast, if the investor holds the shares for just one more day, the tax rate plummets to only 15%. So selling one day too soon could cause the investor to owe 17% more of the profit to the feds. Similarly, the stakes remain high for upper-income investors who can still benefit from a maximum 20% rate on long-term capital gains. For tax-law purposes, the holding period begins the day after investors acquire securities and includes the day they sell. *(IRS Revenue Rulings 66-7, 66-97)* **Example:** Bob buys shares on Sept. 15, 2020. His holding period starts the next day, on Sept. 16. That means Sept. 16, 2021, is the earliest date when Bob can sell and still benefit from the preferential long-term capital gains rate.

- The 25% maximum rate under prior law remains in place for long-term real-estate gains attributable to depreciation. These are so-called unrecaptured Section 1250 gains. Long-term real estate gain over and above the amount of unrecaptured Section 1250 gain is eligible for the 15% rate. The same rules also apply to gains included in deferred installment payments received on or after May 6, 2003.

- The 28% maximum rate under prior law remains in place for long-term gains from collectibles and certain small business stock.

- The reduced capital gains rates have no impact on investments held in traditional IRAs, 401(k) accounts, SEPs and other tax-deferred retirement accounts. Capital gains accumulated in these accounts are still taxed at the investor's regular rate (which can currently be as high as 37%) when withdrawn as cash distributions. Even so, it could still be a tax-smart move for you to use your tax-advantaged retirement accounts to invest in stocks and equity mutual fund shares

Updated tax strategies for capital gain assets

- **Investors should try** hard to satisfy the holding-period rule and keep their shares for more than one year to qualify for the favorable rates on long-term capital gains. The higher an investor's regular tax rate is, the more this rule makes sense. However, it obviously doesn't make sense for investors to put accrued profit at great risk solely to lock in a lower tax rate.

- **When possible, any rapid-fire** stock and mutual fund trading should occur inside tax-advantaged retirement accounts. Then the investor won't be at any tax disadvantage for failing to meet the holding-period rule of more than one year.

- **Investors should hold** equity index mutual funds and tax-efficient funds in their taxable accounts. These funds are less likely to generate ordinary income distributions taxed at higher rates. They can hold mutual funds that engage in rapid-fire churning in tax-advantaged retirement accounts, where such hyperactivity doesn't affect the investor's tax bill.

- **Finally, investors should consider** lightening up on real estate and collectibles. Because of the big difference between paying 28% or 25% and only 15% (or 20% for certain high-income investors), these assets are now somewhat less attractive when compared to stocks. However, real estate still may make sense as part of a fully diversified investment portfolio.

Place optimal assets in retirement and taxable accounts

You may use three types of investment accounts: a Roth IRA, a tax-deferred retirement account (traditional IRA, 401[k], Keogh, etc.) and a taxable brokerage firm account.

Given all the recent tax law changes, which types of investments are best for each type of account? At first glance, you might think it's best to put fixed-income assets into a Roth and tax-deferred accounts because these investments generate highly taxed ordinary income. You could then load up taxable accounts with stocks and index-equity mutual funds that you expect to generate long-term gains and dividends, which will be taxed at the 15% rate (or 20% for certain high-income investors).

In fact, this strategy is part of the current "conventional wisdom," according to many financial media sources. However, we don't believe that the conventional wisdom gets it quite right. To see why, let's make some basic assumptions, crunch some numbers and then compare three investment scenarios for a hypothetical investor named Linda.

Here are the assumptions we'll use:

- **Equity earnings:** Over the long haul, equities will earn 9% annually (pretax). Of that, we assume 6% will be long-term gains from sales of shares held more than one year. The other 3% will come from qualified dividends.

- **Fixed-income investment earnings:** Fixed-income investments (corporate bonds, Treasuries and CDs) will return 5.5% annually (pretax). We assume that all this return will be ordinary income taxed at regular rates when these assets are held in taxable accounts.

- **Tax rate on ordinary income:** Over the next 15 years (until retirement), Linda's combined marginal federal and state tax rate on ordinary income (i.e., her regular rate) will be 38% (combined federal and state).

- **Tax rate gains, dividends:** The combined marginal rate on long-term capital gains and qualified dividends earned in taxable accounts will be only 20% (combined federal and state).

- **Retirement tax rate:** When Linda retires in 15 years, we assume the combined marginal rate on ordinary income then will be 30% (combined federal and state).

- **Investment limits:** Finally, let's assume Linda has $100,000 to invest in the Roth IRA, another $100,000 in the tax-deferred retirement account and $100,000 in a taxable brokerage account ($300,000 total). This asset allocation scheme calls for investing one-third of the money ($100,000) in

fixed-income assets that will generate ordinary income and two-thirds ($200,000) in equities (stocks and equity mutual funds) that will generate capital gains and dividends.

Under this scenario, Linda would have three options for dividing up the $300,000 of investable dough:

- **Option 1:** Allocate the $100,000 of fixed-income investments to the Roth IRA and the $200,000 of equities to tax-deferred retirement and taxable accounts ($100,000 each).

- **Option 2:** Allocate the $100,000 of fixed-income investments to the tax-deferred retirement account and the $200,000 of equities to the Roth and taxable accounts ($100,000 each).

- **Option 3:** Allocate the $100,000 of fixed-income investments to the taxable account and the $200,000 of equities to the tax-deferred retirement and Roth accounts ($100,000 each).

Which option allows Linda to accumulate the most after-tax dollars by the time she retires in 15 years?

Option 1 results (fixed-income investments in Roth IRA). The after-tax value of the Roth IRA will grow to $223,250 ($100,000 invested for 15 years at 5.5% with zero federal or state taxes). The after-tax value of the tax-deferred account is $254,975 ($100,000 invested for 15 years at 9% with 30% of the balance lost to retirement-age taxes). The after-tax value of the taxable account is $283,740 [$100,000 invested for 15 years at an after-tax rate of 7.20% (.80 x 9%)].

Bottom line: Option 1 delivers a total of $761,965 after paying the tax collectors. Not bad, but Linda can do better.

Roth IRA	**$223,250**
Retirement account	**254,975**
Taxable account	**283,740**
Total	**$761,965**

**Option 2 results (fixed-income invest-

ments in tax-deferred account). The after-tax value of the Roth IRA will be $364,250 ($100,000 invested for 15 years at 9% with no taxes). The after-tax value of the tax-deferred account is $156,275 ($100,000 invested for 15 years at 5.5% with 30% lost to retirement-age taxes). The after-tax value of the taxable account is $283,740 [$100,000 invested for 15 years at 7.20% (.80 x 9%)].

Bottom line: Option 2 nets $804,265. That's about $42,000 more than Linda would collect by following Option 1.

Roth IRA	**$364,250**
Retirement account	**156,275**
Taxable account	**283,740**
Total	**$804,265**

Option 3 results (fixed-income investments in taxable account). The after-tax value of the Roth IRA will grow to $364,250 ($100,000 invested for 15 years at 9% with no taxes). The after-tax value of the tax-deferred account is $254,975 ($100,000 invested for 15 years at 9% with 30% lost to retirement-age taxes). The after-tax value of the taxable account is $165,365 [$100,000 invested for 15 years at an after-tax rate of 3.41% (.62 x 5.5%)].

Bottom line: Option 3 yields a total of $784,590.

Roth IRA	**$364,250**
Retirement account	**254,975**
Taxable account	**165,365**
Total	**$784,590**

Tax-smart account allocation conclusions: As you can see, Option 2 works best under our assumptions. Linda would collect about $42,000 more than under Option 1 and about $20,000 more than under Option 3. And all she had to do was vary the accounts used to hold the exact same investments. The differences are due solely to taxes. Taxes really do matter!

Under our assumptions, Option 1 produces by far the worst results. So the first message is simple: Always allocate your Roth IRA balance first to your highest-yielding assets: generally stocks and equity mutual funds. *Don't* dedicate

your Roth balance to lower-yielding, fixed-income investments on the theory of avoiding the higher tax rates that apply to the ordinary income generated by those assets.

As you can see, there isn't a huge difference between Options 2 and 3 under our assumptions. Still, Option 2 comes out ahead by a meaningful amount. However, watch out: The results under Option 2 can be measurably *worse* than under Option 3 if Linda fails to hold equities in the taxable account long enough to qualify for the 15% rate on long-term gains. Ditto if the equity investments are in the form of fast-trading mutual funds, or if the tax rates on capital gains and dividends go back up.

So you probably won't go too far wrong by dedicating your tax-deferred retirement account balance first to equities, even if that pushes some or all of your fixed-income investments into your taxable accounts, where they will generate highly taxed ordinary income. In other words, Option 3 will actually work out better than Option 2 for many folks.

The big exception: if you think that the equity investments will produce almost nothing other than qualified dividends and long-term capital gains taxed at only 15% (or 20% for high-income investors). If you're willing to buy into that giant assumption, Option 2 is probably best for you. In other words, you can dedicate the taxable account balance first to those equity investments that may be taxed at minimal rates, such as equity-index mutual funds and tax-managed funds.

Note: We also ran the numbers using higher and lower tax rates and longer periods until retirement. Our basic conclusions stayed the same.

Don't put variable annuities at top of the list

Variable annuities generally belong near the end of the list of investment alternatives. They're packaged to offer various investment choices similar to what may be obtained with a family of mutual funds.

A big difference: Variable annuities aren't taxed until you withdraw the money. That's great, but all the taxes eventually paid will be at ordinary income rates. And most withdrawals before age 59½ will be subject to an add-on 10% penalty tax to boot.

In contrast, if a person invests in low-turnover mutual funds, a good part of the dividend payouts will probably be taxed at only 15% or 20%, and so will gains on the sale of appreciated shares held over 12 months.

If you die holding a variable annuity contract, your heirs get no tax basis step-up and they'll owe income taxes (at unfavorable ordinary rates) when they withdraw money or liquidate the contract. However, mutual fund shares (as well as stock shares in general) will be stepped up to fair market value at death, so your heirs won't owe capital gains tax when they sell the shares.

Last but not least, most variable annuities charge higher fees and expenses than comparable mutual funds, and they may impose heavy surrender charges if you decide to bail out in the first five or 10 years. It can take decades of successful investing for the tax-deferral advantage of variable annuities to offset the negatives of higher fees and higher tax rates.

Personal residences still look good

From a federal income tax perspective, a home may still be the best investment you can make. The gain-exclusion rule allows most people to avoid federal income taxes completely when they sell at a profit. Gains up to $500,000 are entirely tax-free for married couples who file jointly. The limit is $250,000 for singles and marrieds filing separate status.

What's more, this generous break can be "recycled" every two years. Homeowners can repeatedly buy and sell and merrily reap tax-free gains all the way as long as they owned and used the home in question as the main residence for at least two out of the five years preceding the sale. However, this tax break doesn't apply to "nonqualified" use of a principal residence.

Coverdell education accounts now a better deal

Coverdell Education Savings Accounts (CESAs), formerly known as Education IRAs, have been around for several years. Initially, you could contribute only $500 annually. With that skimpy contribution limit, these accounts weren't really worth the trouble.

However, things have changed a bit, thanks to recent tax legislation. You can now contribute up to $2,000 annually to CESAs. If you have several children (or grandchildren), you can contribute up to $2,000 annually to separate CESAs set up for each one.

CESA earnings are allowed to build up tax-free. Then the money can be withdrawn tax-free to pay the account beneficiary's college expenses. Like contributions to Roth IRAs, contributions to CESAs are nondeductible. But the tax-free withdrawal privilege more than makes up for that.
Bottom line: The $2,000 annual contribution limit has transformed these previously scorned accounts into a more attractive college savings vehicle. The sooner you begin making CESA contributions, the sooner you will begin earning totally tax-free income and gains.

More good news: You can also take tax-free CESA payouts to cover elementary and secondary school (K-12) costs. Under this special privilege, eligible expenses include tuition and fees to attend private and religious schools, plus room and board, uniform and transportation costs. An individual can also withdraw CESA money tax-free to pay out-of-pocket costs to attend public K-12 schools. Eligible expenses include books and supplies; academic tutoring; computers, peripheral equipment and software; and even Internet access charges. It's important to start CESA contributions at an early date to benefit from this break.

Along with numerous other provisions in EGTRRA, the enhancements for CESAs were scheduled to "sunset" after 2012. ATRA permanently extended these for 2013 and thereafter.

One lingering complaint about CESAs: Contributions aren't allowed if the taxpayer's income is too high. However, at least the AGI phaseout range for joint filers was increased several years ago to between $190,000 and $220,000 (up from $150,000 to $160,000). The AGI phase-out range for single, head of household, and married filing separate status remains between $95,000 and $110,000.

What if your income is too high to permit CESA contributions? The best advice: Have someone else who qualifies set up CESAs for the kids. Then give that person (typically a grand-parent or other relative) annual gifts of up to $2,000 for each child to contribute to his CESA.

Build up college savings tax-free with Section 529 plans

Participants in state-sponsored qualified tuition programs, commonly called "Section 529 plans," are also big beneficiaries of EGTRRA. Under these college savings arrangements, parents can fund the account and name a college-bound child as the account beneficiary. Most plans encourage out-of-state investors and accept lump-sum pay-ins of at least $200,000. Or, parents can fund the account in installments.

Most college savings plans also allow several investment options, including equity mutual funds. Withdrawals can be taken to cover college expenses at any accredited institution.

Thanks to EGTRRA, earnings in a Section 529 account are allowed to build up tax-free, and can be withdrawn tax-free to pay college expenses. Originally, the provision allowing tax-free distributions was scheduled to "sunset" after 2010, but TIPRA made it permanent. Also, a provision originally included in the American Recovery and Reinvestment Act (ARRA) permitting tax-free withdrawals to pay for college students' computers or computer technology was made permanent by the PATH Act.

Now the TCJA extends the benefits of Section 529 plans. Beginning in 2018, up to $10,000 of funds may be used to pay tuition at a K-12 private, public or religious school. In addition, the SECURE Act extends this provision to home-schooling expenses, effective in 2020. So 529 plans are no longer just for higher education.

Bottom line: Section 529 plans remain an attractive way for parents to stash away money for college or private school. If you can afford to make substantial contributions to a Section 529 college savings account while your kids are still young, the tax advantages should sharply reduce the amount needed to fully fund their future college educations. The generous tax benefits are available regardless of how high your income may be. In contrast, most of the other education tax breaks aren't available to high-earners.

Custodial accounts for college vs. Section 529 plans

For years, parents put money into custodial accounts for their kids without giving it much thought.

But Section 529 plans may be a viable alternative to such accounts, especially when you weigh the impact of the dreaded "kiddie tax."

Under the kiddie tax, the unearned income a young child receives above an annual threshold is subject to the kiddie tax. For 2020, the first $1,100 is exempt from tax, and the next $1,100 is taxed at 10%. Any amount above the $2,200 total is taxed at a higher rate.

Prior to 2018, the kiddie tax rate was based on the top tax of the child's parents. Under a provision in the TCJA, the excess was to be taxed under the rate structure in effect for estates and trusts. But the SECURE Act repeals this provision, so the excess is still taxed at the parents' top rate. The "fix" is effective for 2020 and thereafter, but can be elected retroactive to 2018.

Also, before 2006, the kiddie tax applied only to children under age 14. TIPRA raised the limit to age 18 for the 2006 tax year. Then, the "small business law" raised the bar again. Beginning in 2008, the kiddie tax applies to children who are under age 19 or full-time students under age 24 who don't have earned income exceeding half their support.

Key point: Unlike the income generated by custodial accounts, earnings in a 529 plan don't count toward the kiddie tax. That, along with the state income-tax incentives afforded to 529s, gives these plans a major advantage.

Another downside to the custodial account idea: The child gains unfettered access to the account balance when he reaches age 18 or 21 (depending on state law). Why? Because the money in a custodial account legally belongs to the child. As custodian over the account, a parent can supervise the money only until the child reaches the age of majority. After that, the parent loses all control.

Give securities to child to finance college education

The 2003 Tax Act reduced the federal income tax rate on long-term capital gains to only 5% for those in the 10% or 15% rate bracket. The 5% rate dropped to zero for 2008 through 2012. ATRA permanently extended the zero percent rate for 2013 and thereafter. So now it's smarter than ever for high-bracket members of the older generation to give away appreciated securities to their children and grandchildren in the low tax brackets.

As long as the combined holding periods for donor and the child (the donee or the gift recipient) add up to more than one year, the child can sell the appreciated securities and pay zero percent tax on the resulting long-term capital gains. The child also pays zero percent federal income tax on qualified dividends collected after receiving gifts of dividend-paying stock.

Accordingly, you could transfer stock to a child in a low tax bracket. The transfer is sheltered from the annual gift tax exclusion ($15,000 per recipient for 2020). If your child sells the stock in 2020, he or she pays zero tax on the gain, so long as your combined holding period is more than one year.

But don't forget about potential kiddie tax complications.

Thus, your overall tax strategy depends on the age of your child in 2020:

- **If your child will be under age 18:** Any capital gains are subject to the kiddie tax, so try to keep your child's unearned income below or close to the $2,200 level.

- **If your child will be between the ages of 18 and 24:** The kiddie tax may apply if your child is either under age 19 or a full-time student under age 24. Generally, this includes children who can be claimed as your dependents. Figure out the ramifications of large capital gains.

- **If your child will be age 24 or older:** Feel free to have your child sell securities in 2020 to benefit from the zero percent rate. This assumes your child will have little other income this year.

Pocket $3,000 each December

Near the end of every year, investors should check their capital gains and losses to see where they stand. They may want to avoid net capital gains because they'll owe tax the following April. However, if an investor has too many capital losses, she will have to carry them forward, without taking deductions. Carry-forwards may last for many years, giving no payoff.

The ideal situation is to wind up with a net $3,000 capital loss each year because that's the maximum that can be deducted. So, if you have excess losses, it's advisable to take gains in December. The cash you receive will be sheltered by losses already taken.

If you have net gains, you can sell losers to get down to a $3,000 loss. Then you can buy back the same securities 31 days later. Or, you can buy similar, but not identical, securities right away.

A $3,000 capital loss provides a $3,000 deduction. If your tax bracket (including state and local income taxes) is 33% or higher, that's like putting an extra $1,000 or more in your pocket each year.

Cope with 3.8% Medicare surtax

As if all the recent tax law changes weren't enough to make your head spin, certain high-income investors have to contend with yet another tax wrinkle.

Beginning in 2013, the PPACA health care reform law imposed a 3.8% Medicare surtax on the *lesser* of "net investment income" (NII) or the amount by which modified AGI exceeds $200,000 for single filers and $250,000 for joint filers. For estates and trusts, the surtax applies to the *lesser* of undistributed NII or AGI above the dollar amount beginning in the highest tax bracket.

For this purpose, NII includes interest, dividends, capital gains, rents, royalties, nonqualified annuities, income from passive activities, and income from the trading of financial instruments or commodities. But certain other items are excluded from the definition of NII, including wages, self-employment income, Social Security benefits, tax-exempt interest, gains from the sale of a principal residence up to the amount of the tax exclusion, operating income from a non-passive business and distributions from qualified retirement plans.

Example: Joshua, a single filer, has an annual modified AGI of $300,000. He realizes $50,000 of NII in 2020. Because the NII of $50,000 is less than the excess $100,000 of modified AGI above the $200,000 threshold, Joshua must pay a surtax of $1,900 (3.8% of $50,000), in addition to regular income tax.

The impact of this tax law change, combined with other effective tax rate increases for high-income investors, can be significant. It can hike your top 2020 tax rate on some income to as high as 40.8% (37% + 3.8%)—not even counting any state and local income taxes!

Nevertheless, you can counteract the 3.8% Medicare surtax with astute planning. Here are several possible suggestions.

5 ways to defuse the surtax

1. **Don't be passive about investments.** Net investment income includes amounts generated by passive activities such as rental real estate. Therefore, if you own a business interest where you don't take on an active management role, you might get socked with the extra tax liability. Conversely, if you "materially participate" in the business, the income generally won't count as NII. *Caveat:* Special rules apply to rental real estate.

2. **Add munis to your portfolio.** The income from municipal bonds ("munis"), or certain municipal bond funds, is completely exempt from federal income tax. Therefore, buying more munis won't result in the extra tax on NII.

3. **Bulk up your 401(k) account.** Distributions from a qualified retirement plan, like a 401(k), don't count as NII. Therefore, the more you can put away in your 401(k) plan (within the generous tax law limits), the more you can shelter from the extra Medicare surtax. At the same time, you're setting aside funds that can grow on a tax-deferred basis until you're ready to retire.

4. **Switch to a Roth IRA.** Although traditional IRA distributions aren't treated as NII, they can still increase your modified AGI in a year in which the surtax applies. *Better idea:* Start contributing to a Roth to build up a nest egg that can eventually be tapped tax-free. However, if you convert some or all of your funds in existing IRAs into a Roth, you'll owe current tax on the conversion.

5. **Set up a charitable remainder trust (CRT).** This wealth transfer strategy was valuable prior to imposition of the surtax. Typically, you receive a charitable deduction for transferring property to the CRT, which pays out income over time. Then the pre-designated charity receives the remainder. This technique may enable you to keep your income below the surtax threshold for the years of the trust's term.

Remember to coordinate your efforts to minimize or avoid the 3.8% Medicare surtax with other tax aspects. You can't make these decisions in a vacuum.

7. Finding Opportunities in Real Estate

Unfortunately, fewer tax shelters are available in real estate today than during the 1980s. Nowadays, depreciation benefits are smaller, and losses aren't always deductible.

Nevertheless, many tax-saving opportunities in real estate still exist for those who know where to look for them. Real estate markets vary, so you may be able to find good properties at attractive prices. Tax breaks can help investors hold on until the market turns up and those properties appreciate.

Fortunes have been made in real estate throughout this nation's history. We've no reason to think the future will be any different even though real estate prices may decline from time to time.

Own or rent business premises?

Once your company's profits begin growing and the business stabilizes, you might consider owning the quarters rather than renting.

To evaluate the comparative costs of doing so, consider a reasonable length of time, such as 10 years. Include in the calculations the purchase price of a quality building at the desired location. The cost of the building can be depreciated ("improvements") but not the cost of the land. Add together the cost of financing 100% of the purchase price at the prevailing interest rate, maintenance costs, straight-line depreciation and property taxes. The total of these items is the "rent equivalent."

Compare this cost figure with projected rental costs for 10 years and factor in expected rent increases (2-4% per year is usually realistic). Don't overlook the company's future expansion needs. Whether you buy or rent, you must be able to expand or contract space as needed. If you plan to own your space, you may consider buying a larger building and renting out part of the space on a short-term basis.

Slash taxes via 'private arrangement'

Suppose you decide to own rather than rent business property. In that case, you have another decision to make: Who should own the real estate: you or the corporation?

Usually, it's better to own the real estate and lease it to the company if it's a C corporation. The corporation probably can receive a full deduction for the lease payments it makes to you. This will reduce the corporate income tax it has to pay.

At the same time, if you own the building, you can depreciate it. The depreciation deductions can offset all or part of the rental income received. If you wind up with a net loss from the property, it might be deductible; even if that's not possible, you might be able to deduct payments for real estate taxes and mortgage interest.

Plus, if the building appreciates, it's easier to cash in on gains (refinancing, property sale) without adverse tax results if you hold it personally rather than through a corporation.

Shelter up to $25,000 per year

Real estate prices are down in many areas of the country, so some excellent buying opportunities are out there. In addition, investors still have some real estate tax shelters.

Directly owned real estate

You can find tax shelter in investment property, ranging from a house or condo that you rent out to a shopping center owned with a few associates. However, you must clear a row of obstacles before you can take deductions.

An investor must own at least 10% of the property, and you generally can't own the property through a limited partnership interest. Also, you have to "actively manage" the property. That doesn't mean replacing faulty fuses or switches. You can hire a property manager and a rental agent, but you must participate in management decisions, such as tenant selection and capital improvements, and must keep records to show your participation.

More obstacles relate to income. Say your adjusted gross income is lower than $100,000 per year; you can deduct up to $25,000 worth of losses per year. However, if your AGI is more than $100,000, the allowable deduction declines to zero at $150,000. For example, with an AGI of $125,000, Melissa can deduct $12,500 worth of losses from directly owned real estate. (Even if her AGI is more than $150,000, she still may deduct some losses if they're used to offset "passive income," perhaps those from another real estate venture.)

In depressed real estate markets, you may well find sound real estate at bargain prices. The tax break will help you hold on until the market turns up.

Historic rehabs

Another investing tip: Prior to 2018, you could earn a 10% tax credit for fixing up old buildings, 20% if the building was "historic." The requirements for historic properties are more liberal than you might think. It doesn't mean George Washington had to have slept there; the building may be indicative of a certain type of architecture at a specific period in time.

To qualify for the historic credit, the building must be listed on the National Register of Historic Places or located in a registered historic district and certified by the Secretary of the Interior as being historically significant.

The TCJA eliminates the 10% rehab credit, but retains the 20% credit for historic structures. However, the credit must now be claimed ratably over a five-year period.

Low-income housing

To encourage the building and rehabilitation of apartments for low-income renters, the federal government provides tax credits.

A number of low-income housing partnerships are on the market now; minimum investments are as low as $5,000. In general, for each $5,000 invested, an investor can expect about

$7,500 in tax savings, spread over a period of 10 years. Then the partnership must hold its properties for another five years before disposing of them. No income limits apply. Tax credits are practically limited to $8,750 per year; that's the equivalent of sheltering $25,000 in income per year in a 35% tax bracket.

What a low-income housing project will be worth at the time of sale is unknown. Investors can hope that new tax-shelter investors will be encouraged to come in, giving them a return of capital. If so, the total return may be nearly 15% per year after taxes.

IRS rules ensure tax-deferred real estate exchanges

For real estate investors with big gains, selling leads to high federal taxes. Add the cost of state and local taxes and the total tab may exceed 30% for high-income taxpayers.

To escape a big tax hit, many investors will "trade" instead, based on the favorable tax rules for like-kind exchanges. Previously, tax benefits were available for several types of business or investment properties, but the TCJA limits the use of like-kind exchanges to real estate, beginning in 2018.

Suppose you're moving to a different part of the country. Maybe you want a property that produces more current cash flow, or one that the banks are more likely to allow borrowing money against.

When real estate is exchanged, the owner owes no tax, even if the property's value has increased. Suppose Carolyn bought a small apartment building in Philadelphia many years ago for $500,000, and it's now appraised at $900,000. She trades it for an apartment building in Orlando, also appraised at $900,000. She'll pay no tax on the $400,000 difference. (Receiving cash or enjoying a reduction in outstanding debt will result in a taxable gain.)

Over the years, IRS rulings and court decisions have broadened the scope of "like-kind" to include almost any type of real estate.

Carolyn could swap her Philadelphia apartment house for a shopping center, a marina, raw land and so forth. If she has several properties adding up to a $900,000 value, she could swap them for one $900,000 property, or vice versa.

Moreover, you don't have to swap real estate like you'd trade baseball cards. Most real estate exchanges these days are "Starker" exchanges, named after a landmark court decision in the late 1970s. Starker exchanges typically are three-party deals, with a delay between transactions.

Suppose Carolyn sells her apartment building to Joe for $900,000. Several months later, she uses that $900,000 to buy raw land from Jan. The net effect is that Carolyn owns raw land instead of an apartment building, and she owes no taxes.

That's where IRS regulations come in. They spell out the procedures that you must follow to implement a deferred three-party, like-kind exchange, and they provide a "safe harbor."

The regs spell out how to identify the property acquired in an exchange. This identification must be made within 45 days after the investor sells the original property. The identification must be in writing and be delivered (mail or fax is OK) to an unrelated party who's involved in the transaction.

The IRS regs permit an investor to identify three properties of any value so she can keep her options open. Or, the investor can identify many properties, as long as their combined value is no more than 200% of the value of the property/properties sold.

In deferred exchanges, money can't be held between transactions. The original sales proceeds must be held in escrow, again by an unrelated party, until the replacement property is purchased. In our $900,000 example, Carolyn wouldn't actually get her hands on the cash from the apartment building sale. The IRS regs say that it's OK to protect cash while it's in escrow with a letter of credit or some other type of guarantee. The IRS will even permit taxpayers to earn interest on it in the interim.

So-called "accommodators" will hold the money during a Starker exchange and then spend it to purchase the replacement property. The investor then acquires the replacement property by making a like-kind exchange with the accommodator. This is a three-party transaction: the investor, the accommodator and the person who sells the replacement property to the accommodator. Since the investor ends up swapping property for property with no cash received, this qualifies for tax-free exchange treatment on the investor's end. She pays the accommodator a fee, but probably one that's less than the interest earned while she has parked the funds with him.

The acquisition of the replacement property must take place within 180 days of the disposition of the first, or by the due date of the tax return (including extensions) for the year of the exchange, whichever comes first.

Like-kind exchange properties must be intended for investment or use in a trade or business. For example, you can't exchange a personal vacation residence for another and expect tax-free treatment. And while reducing debt will result in taxable gain, you can leverage up if you want. As is the case with all real estate, if exchanged property is owned at death, your heirs will get a step-up in basis. That means they'll owe no capital gains tax on all the appreciation that took place in those properties during your lifetime.

8. Get More Mileage From Travel Deductions

In the past, the IRS closely scrutinized deductions claimed for travel and entertainment (T&E) expenses. But now the deduction for entertainment expenses has been repealed by the TCJA, beginning in 2018. Also, the deduction for miscellaneous expenses, including unreimbursed employee business expenses like travel expenses incurred on behalf of a company, has been eliminated for 2018 through 2025.

Business travel expenses, however, remain deductible, so the IRS will likely continue its close examination of small businesses' expense accounts because it considers this an extremely lucrative area for revenue enhancement. Still, there is some room to claim certain tax breaks. This chapter outlines areas where you can maximize the available tax benefits remaining on the books.

Let the company pick up the tab

In the best of all possible worlds, a business owner can charge all his travel costs to the company. The company will get deductions for the expenses, and the owner doesn't pick up any taxable income.

Unfortunately, that's not often how it works. The IRS may well say that the travel was a personal benefit, so the individual is socked with a tax bill.

Fortunately, you can shift travel costs to the company if you follow the rules:

- **If a trip is primarily** for business, the entire transportation expense is deductible. That includes meals (limited to 50% of the cost), lodging, phone calls and other expenses attributable to business activities at the destination.

- **Even if a trip is primarily** for pleasure, business side-trip costs are deductible.

  Observation: If you keep good records

and can show that a trip was primarily for business, the deduction will stand up.

However, a tougher standard applies for business owners traveling outside the United States. If a trip lasts more than a week and personal activities occupy more than 25% of the time, travel expenses must be allocated according to the time spent on business; only the business portion will be deductible.

Previously, similar rules applied to deductions for business entertaining. Meals with customers and clients, for example, had to have a clear business purpose, with substantial business discussions before, during or following the meal. The same held true for taking a business associate to a sports event or a play, for example. Deductions for those expenses were limited to 50% of the cost.

Now the TCJA completely eliminates deductions for entertainment expenses, beginning in 2018. However, you can still write off 50% of the cost of meals while traveling away from home on business. In addition, as we will see later, you may also derive benefits from certain other food and beverage expenses.

Maximize write-offs for mixing business with pleasure

You can deduct costs incurred in traveling away from home, local travel while away from home, meals and lodging; such deductions are allowed for business or investment purposes as long as the expenses are "ordinary and necessary." For example, both the Tax Court and the IRS have agreed that travel away from home to look after income-producing property is deductible. If you take a cab to visit your broker for a consultation, that expense is deductible as well.

Similarly, for those who travel abroad seeking foreign markets for goods or services, the travel costs can be deducted as long as they're not lavish.

However, investment seminars and conventions are no longer deductible. Nor is travel as a form of education (e.g., if someone teaches Spanish, that person can't deduct a trip to Spain on the grounds that it will improve her language skills).

Wrap personal days around business travel (or vice versa)

We all know that vacation expenses generally aren't deductible. But what if an employee combines business travel with vacation days? As long as the primary reason for a domestic trip is business, transportation costs (plane, train or automobile) will always qualify for deductions, even if the employee pursues personal interests after arriving there. Of course, there are limits. If the employee is ever audited on the issue, the IRS will compare time spent on business versus vacationing, so it's crucial to keep careful records of all business-related time and expenses.

Example: David arranges a meeting with an client in Dallas on a Tuesday. He and his spouse fly out Saturday morning and leave early Wednesday. The meeting clearly necessitated the trip, and David didn't spend an unreasonable amount of time vacationing. He can deduct his airline ticket (but generally not his spouse's), the meal and lodging (within the usual limits) for Monday night and his out-of-pocket expenses for Tuesday. If the meeting lasts most of Tuesday, he can deduct that night's lodging as well.

Sometimes, it's just not possible to justify the trip as being primarily for business. For example, one week working out of town and three weeks playing generally means no travel deductions because vacation considerations clearly outweigh business concerns. However, even in such circumstances you can still deduct the business expenses incurred at the out-of-town location: auto mileage or rental car, parking, lodging for the night before a meeting, meals, copying, phone calls, faxes, etc.

If an employer reimburses business travel costs, it's not taxable income to the employee provided she's required to account properly for those expenses. The company will be limited to a 50% deduction for meal outlays.

Have Uncle Sam foot the bill with Saturday night stay-over

Do you want more than just partial write-offs when you mix business and pleasure? Even the IRS agrees there's a way to deduct all expenses with no questions asked. The trick is to use a Saturday night stay-over to reduce the overall cost of a business trip. If you can show the airfare savings offset the costs of staying for the extra personal days, you can go ahead and deduct all the expenses. Of course, you must have a dominant business purpose for the trip.

Example: Susan schedules a business meeting in New York on Monday morning. She and her spouse fly in Friday night and spend the weekend on the town. On Monday, she attends the meeting and returns home that night. Let's assume the round-trip airfare is only $400 versus $1,100 if she came in Sunday and left Monday. As long as the expenses for the personal days (Friday and Saturday) are less than $700, Susan can justify writing off all her travel, meal and lodging (subject to the 50% limit on meals). However, you generally can't deduct expenses for a spouse (such as airfare and meals and any extra charge for a double room), and there's no write-off for purely personal items, such as play tickets and cab fares to tourist spots.

In using the Saturday night stay-over scheme, make sure that you nail down your deductions by carefully documenting the airfare savings and comparing them to the cost of staying the extra days.

Travel expenses for spouse or companion

Travel costs for a spouse or a companion generally aren't deductible unless the person is an employee of the firm and has an independent business reason for making the trip.

Of course, if a spouse or companion is an employee of another company, that employer can deduct the expenses if the trip has a business purpose for it.

Also, if a spouse or companion is self-employed in her own business and has a business reason for making the trip, expenses can be written off. For example, say you make a business trip to Europe on behalf of your company and your self-employed spouse makes the same trip with the legitimate purpose of visiting existing customers and drumming up new business. Both you and your spouse can write off your respective travel expenses in such situations.

IRS dishes out tax break for meals

Fortunately, the IRS has provided a way to get around the TCJA crackdown on entertainment and meal expenses. According to a Notice issued in 2018 (Notice 2018-76), you still may deduct 50% of the cost of certain meals, despite the recent tax law changes.

Prior to 2018, you could deduct 50% of the cost of qualified entertainment expenses that were properly substantiated. This included entertainment that was "directly-related" to or "associated with" the business. For instance, deductions were allowed for meals in a clear business setting, like a hospitality suite at a convention, as well as meals directly following or preceding a "substantial business discussion."

But the 50% deduction for meals was limited to costs that were not considered "lavish or extravagant" under the circumstances. Plus, you or someone representing your business had to be present when the food and beverages were served.

Beginning in 2018, the TCJA repeals the deduction for entertainment expenses. Initially, many tax experts thought this also wiped out the deduction for meals incurred in connection with entertainment.

Notice 2018-76 indicates that taxpayers may deduct 50% of the cost of business meals if:

- The expense is an ordinary and necessary business expense paid or incurred during the tax year.

- The expense is not lavish or extravagant under the circumstances.

- The taxpayer, or an employee of the taxpayer, is present when the food or beverages are furnished.

- The food and beverages are provided to a current or potential business customer, client, consultant or similar business contact.

- For food and beverages provided during or at an entertainment activity, they are purchased separately from the entertainment or the cost of the food and beverages is stated separately from the cost of the entertainment on one or more bills, invoices or receipts.

Caveat: You can't circumvent the rules by inflating amounts charged for food and beverages in connection with entertainment activities. The IRS says this is a no-no.

To further illustrate the new rules, the IRS provided three examples in the 2018 Notice where business taxpayers attended games with business contacts.

Example 1: Ed takes a customer to a baseball game and buys the hot dogs and drinks. The tickets are nondeductible entertainment, but Ed can deduct 50% of the cost of the hot dogs and drinks purchased separately.

Example 2: Kate takes a customer to a basketball game in a luxury suite. During the game, they have access to food and beverages, which are included in the cost of the tickets. Both the cost of the tickets and the food and beverages are nondeductible entertainment.

Example 3: The same as in Example 2, except that the invoice for the basketball game tickets separately states the cost of the food and beverages. In this case, Kate can deduct 50% of the cost of the food and beverages.

Note: You can rely on the 2018 Notice until the IRS issues proposed regulations.

Back up travel deductions with receipts

To support your travel deductions for 2020 you should have records showing:

- Amount of each separate expenditure.

- Dates of the trip and number of days spent

on business.

- Travel destinations.
- Business reasons for travel.

To support your meal deductions, records should show:

- Amount of each separate expenditure.
- Date of meal.
- Location (e.g., dinner at Tony's).

- Business purpose of meal.
- Names and occupations of the attendees, showing the business relationship.

Receipts or similar evidence generally are necessary to support all travel and meal expenses of $75 or more. Taxpayers must keep receipts for lodging expenses even if they are less than $75.

9. Fine Points: Tax Havens

Advance tax planning is essential to realize the most savings possible. Because repetitive tax changes have become the norm rather than the exception, you need to stay up to date with all the changes the IRS has implemented or is contemplating.

This chapter explains certain areas that have become ambiguous because of IRS reform yet can still provide some of the best tax-saving opportunities for you.

Supershelter: Open a charitable remainder trust

A charitable remainder trust (CRT) sounds like a simple vehicle. The donor gives assets to a trust, the trust pays income for a certain period, and the charity keeps whatever's left. Typically, the donor (variously called the maker, creator or grantor of the trust) receives income for the rest of his life, as well as possibly for his spouse's life. So where's the tax shelter? First, let's start with the estate tax shelter.

Anything donated to a CRT is removed from the creator's taxable estate as well as the spouse's estate. They pay no gift tax on charitable contributions, no matter how large.

Second, there's an immediate income tax benefit. Say you give $1 million to a CRT. At some point, that $1 million (either increased by investment earnings or reduced by distributions) will go to a hospital, university, charity and so forth that you name. Your tax adviser can calculate the value of the future contribution using IRS tables. Then, that projected future gift can be discounted to a present value, which you can deduct if you're an itemizer.

For example, a $1 million gift today might yield a $250,000 income tax deduction. There are limits on the amount of charitable contributions that you can deduct in one year, but excess amounts can be carried forward for up to five years.

(By law, a CRT donor can take a fixed income each year, no less than 5% of the original donation, or a variable income, no less than 5% of the annual valuation. The older the donor is and the less income he agrees to take out of the trust, the greater the upfront income tax deduction will be.)

Third, there's a capital gains tax break. If someone donates appreciated assets to the trust, the trust can sell them. Because a CRT is tax exempt, the capital gains obligation disappears.

Let's say that Joe owns stock he bought for $100,000, now worth $1 million. The stock pays no dividend and he'd like to increase his income. If Joe sold it outright, he'd have a $900,000 capital gain, which means the IRS coffers would be enriched by $180,000 at the 20% long-term capital gains rate. That would leave Joe with $720,000 to invest; in 5% Treasuries, he'd receive $36,000 per year.

Instead, Joe decides to donate the stock to a CRT, which sells the stock for $1 million and has the entire amount to reinvest because it's tax exempt. Now, there's $1 million to invest in 5% Treasuries, yielding $50,000 per year. That money all can go to Joe for as long as he lives.

If you look hard at the CRT structure, you'll see that there are some losers: Joe's heirs, probably his children. If he had held onto the $1 million worth of stock, they would have inherited all of it with no estate taxes due. But since the stock has been donated to the charitable trust, the heirs will receive nothing.

Assuming Joe is still insurable, he might buy life insurance. In our example, where he gets a $250,000 tax deduction, he could save perhaps $100,000 in taxes. That $100,000 can be put toward a permanent life insurance policy, say, for $500,000. So the kids reap some benefit from the deal and Joe gets higher lifetime income.

Finally, be aware of another requirement for CRTs: For those created after June 27, 2005, a donor must obtain a signed waiver from his spouse in order to preserve the tax benefits of the trust. The IRS has imposed this new rule to avoid potential conflicts under state laws.

Beat the IRS in divorce matters

Under prior law, if you paid alimony to a divorced or separated spouse, you could deduct those payments on your personal tax return, while the payments constituted table income to the recipient. However, payments qualified as deductible alimony only if all of the following requirements were met:

- The spouses don't file a joint return with each other.

- The payment is in cash or a cash-equivalent.

- The payment is to or for a spouse or a former spouse made under a divorce or separation instrument.

- The divorce or separation instrument doesn't designate the payment as not alimony.

- The spouses aren't members of the same household when the payment is made.

- There's no liability to make the payment after the death of the recipient spouse.

On the other hand, payments for child support or property settlements were not deductible, nor were they taxable to the recipient.

The TCJA repeals the deduction for alimony payments by payors, and the corresponding taxation of payments by recipients for agreements executed after December 31, 2018. However, alimony paid under pre-2019 agreements remains deductible by payors and taxable to recipients. Finally, note that the TCJA provisions for alimony are permanent.

Avert IRS showdown: Create a clean buy-sell

A buy-sell agreement is a must for any business owner. It's a formal agreement spelling out who will take over the company when the owner leaves. With a buy-sell, the owner knows how much she's going to collect and when. The owner might, for example, retire at age 65 and

sell the company on the installment plan, payable over five years.

To satisfy IRS rules, buy-sell agreements must be:

- **Bona fide.**

- **Not a device to transfer** a business for less than its full value.

- **Comparable to similar** arrangements entered into at arm's length.

Essentially, those are three ways of saying the same thing. The law simply says that a buy-sell agreement must have a legitimate valuation to pass IRS scrutiny. Why the fuss? Small companies, especially those passed from one family member to another, have tried to low-ball their buy-sell valuations to cut estate taxes.

What happens without a buy-sell? The family inherits the owner's interest in the business. If no one in the family can take over, the estate will have to sell to a co-owner or to another buyer for the highest bid. At that point, the family will be negotiating from weakness. Plus, if the owner has been the driving force behind the company, her absence may leave the company much less attractive to a new buyer.

If there's an anointed successor in the family, the main problem is estate tax. At the owner's death, the executor will put a value on the company and file an estate tax return, based on that valuation. The IRS generally takes a hard look at such returns; the valuation may well be challenged.

For simplicity, say a business owner died in 2020 with a remaining estate tax exemption of $5 million. An executor puts a $5 million value on the business, but upon review the IRS says it's worth $5.5 million. The difference: $175,000 in estate taxes, plus interest. The estate can fight the IRS and thus incur attorney's fees with no certainty of prevailing. Or, the estate may be able to settle for some number in between, probably a fairly hefty sum. So leaving the business to a successor in the family would likely lead to an expensive, time-consuming dispute with the IRS.

An owner can short-circuit that clash with

a buy-sell agreement. At the owner's death, the successor is obliged to buy the interest from the estate at an agreed-upon price.

As long as the successor is an unrelated party (a co-owner, say, or an employee), there should be no problem. With conflicting interests, both sides negotiate to make the best deal possible. The resulting price will be fair, in most circumstances. Therefore, the IRS will accept the buy-sell price as a valuation of the company for estate tax purposes.

However, the same rules don't apply when the buy-sell involves members of the same family. If Mom is going to sell her business to her son, rather than leave it to him at her death, there's no guarantee that the price will be fair. What's to stop Mom from putting a $5 million price tag on a company that's really worth $5.5 million if her son is the buyer? From the viewpoint of the IRS, that's a device for evading estate tax.

That's why Congress was so insistent on fair valuations in buy-sell agreements that it repeated the point three times in a law passed in 1990. If you play it straight with a realistic valuation, the estate will have a relatively easy time. But if a skimpy price is established, the IRS has statutory authority to throw out the valuation and come in with its own. Then it's up to the estate to prove that the IRS is wrong.

Out of harm's way

How can a business owner keep the estate out of trouble? You can arrange to have a formal buy-sell, drawn up by a respected attorney, including a valuation by a reputable outsider, such as your tax adviser.

You have any number of ways to handle a valuation. The buy-sell could call for an annual appraisal provided by a respected CPA firm. It might be based on a formula, such as 10 times net operating income. Or, you may use an executor to fix a valuation at the date of your death (and on the "alternative valuation date," six months later).

In any event, you should use a credible professional with no family ties and no conflicts of interest. The more prestigious the name

on the appraisal, the harder for the IRS to say the valuation isn't bona fide.

Does that mean that buy-sells between unrelated parties are carefree? No, although there are fewer IRS worries, the IRS may still be concerned about the buyer's good faith. Suppose a buyout is to be funded with life insurance. What's to stop the buyer from skipping a premium or two or borrowing against the cash value? In that case, the full life insurance won't be available when it's needed.

The answer: Sophisticated sellers create a trust to hold the policy. When the owner dies, the life insurance proceeds will be paid to the trust, which can buy the shares from the estate.

Why do you need a trust? A properly executed buy-sell agreement is enforceable, but there's always a temptation when someone receives hundreds of thousands of dollars in life insurance proceeds. The buyer may try to delay the purchase or stretch it out. In the meantime, that money is exposed to other creditors. Your heirs may be forced into litigation to get the money, and that can cause even greater delays.

Suppose the value of your business outstrips the amount of life insurance. That's another benefit of using a trust. If, for example, the insurance proceeds are enough to buy 60% of the shares in question, the trustee would pay the proceeds to the heirs and release 60% of the shares to the buyer. A good buy-sell agreement will include a payment schedule for the remaining shares—payable over four years, perhaps, with 10% interest due on the unpaid balance. The money might come from the business's ongoing revenues, with the trustee releasing shares as payments come in. Again, your family is more likely to be fully protected if there's a trust to ensure the buy-sell is carried out per the agreement.

Hire independent contractors

Many companies, large and small, use independent contractors rather than employees for some jobs. They can provide flexibility, cut costs and reduce paperwork. If you aren't careful about how you use contractors, however, you may face a hassle with the IRS.

Independent contractors may not have to be included in fringe benefit coverage, including retirement plans. (Make sure their contracts spell that out.) But the big advantage in using them is in the area of payroll taxes. For employees, you must withhold part of each paycheck, match the withheld portion and send both sums to the IRS. There's also the accounting time and costs involved.

For independent contractors, compensation is simpler. The employer sends checks to the workers. At the end of each year, employers send information reports (Form 1099) to the contract workers and to the IRS.

The IRS, however, prefers that employers classify workers as employees rather than independent contractors because it likes to have payroll taxes withheld. That way, the money comes into the agency automatically and on time. Therefore, if there's any doubt at all, the IRS will likely recharacterize independent contractors as employees.

The IRS has established general guidelines covering who's an employee and who's a contract worker. If a company has been paying workers as independent contractors but the IRS claims that they're really employees, the company will owe back taxes, interest and penalties.

How can you tell the difference between a contractor and an employee? The most important factor is control. If an employer has the right to control how and when someone works, that person is most likely an employee.

Another important factor is a worker's risk of loss. A person who pays none of his own business expenses and is guaranteed regular compensation is likely to be considered an employee; one who pays some expenses, with uncertain earnings prospects, is probably an independent contractor.

Finally, consider the impact of the deduction for pass-through entities created by the TCJA. Workers who are treated as independent contractors may reap tax benefits on their personal tax returns. *(See Chapter 3.)*

Drill for deep tax shelter in oil and gas

In drilling funds, investors pool their money, which is used by a driller to hunt for oil, natural gas or both.

As is the case with other types of partnerships, public drilling funds are composed of thousands of investors who contribute tens of millions of dollars to drill in several places. In private drilling funds, a few wealthy investors make larger commitments, but the total amount raised winds up being smaller.

In either case, investors may benefit from two prime tax shelters:

- **In the first year or two,** from a deduction for intangible drilling costs (IDC).

- **Over the life of the venture,** from an allowance for "percentage" depletion.

The net result: You may get a large upfront deduction to shelter other income. And ongoing revenues from selling the oil and gas will be partially sheltered from taxation. Thanks to a special provision in the tax code regarding the deduction for intangible drilling costs, oil and gas investors can deduct most of their drilling costs upfront.

Example: Oil Drilling Fund raises $10 million. After all costs, $8.5 million is spent on drilling the first year. Of that $8.5 million, $8 million is deductible, thanks to the IDC. Normally, it takes awhile for oil and gas to be "lifted" and sold. Thus, Oil Drilling may have no income in its first year. With $8 million in tax deductions and zero in income, it reports an $8 million loss for the year.

That loss is passed through to investors, who put up the $10 million. Thus, each investor can report a loss of 80% of his contribution. A $10,000 investor would get an $8,000 tax loss. However, to get the initial write-off, individuals can't invest as limited partners. Many drilling funds are now structured so that investors are general partners, or investors may enter into a joint venture.

So you have to take risks to get drilling fund deductions. Theoretically, you're exposed to all the obligations of the drilling fund. If some kind of drilling disaster occurs, you could be liable for damage awards.

In a good drilling fund, the sponsor will do as much as possible to reduce those risks. A multimillion-dollar insurance policy will be in place; someone else will put his assets on the line before those of the investors. Probably, there will be a plan for investors to convert to limited partners after the drilling is done and tax deductions are no longer needed.

What if you don't want to assume the extra liability? You can invest as a limited partner. As such, you're participating in a passive activity and can't deduct the losses immediately unless you have passive income from other sources. Instead, the losses will be carried forward to offset income from the drilling fund. Thanks to the loss carry-forward, all the drilling fund income may be sheltered for several years.

You can expect first-year write-offs of anywhere from 50% to 90% of your investment. In some deals, payments for the investment are made over several years.

If the drilling is successful, revenues will start to flow to investors. That's where percentage depletion comes in. If new oil and gas is discovered, you can deduct 15% of the gross revenues. That's what's meant by percentage depletion. You might wind up sheltering 20% to 25% of your drilling fund net revenues.

Percentage depletion continues as long as you're receiving income. You may, in time, shelter more income than the amount you actually invested.

Increase retirement shelter: Use a defined-benefit plan

After all the "tax reform" during the past few years, one shelter has emerged virtually unscathed: qualified retirement plans. A company can make tax-deductible contributions to the plan on behalf of its employees. Inside the plan, the money will grow untaxed until it's withdrawn.

Among retirement plans, defined-benefit plans may offer the most tax shelter. Such plans are designed by an actuary or a pension consultant (perhaps you can also provide this type of service). Based on age, salary and years of service, a monthly income will be set for each employee. The consultant determines how much is contributed to receive that benefit upon the employee's retirement.

This kind of plan is especially attractive for business owners and executives who are in their 50s and have relatively few years to build up retirement funds. The company may be able to contribute (and deduct) tens of thousands of dollars a year or more on the owner's behalf. The owner may double or triple the retirement benefits, compared with what he could receive using other types of retirement plans.

Say a business owner has $200,000 worth of net earnings. If she's eligible to contribute $40,000 this year to the plan, that would reduce taxable income to $150,000. The other $40,000 will continue to compound for the owner, tax deferred.

Defined-benefit plans may work particularly well if your employees tend to be young and low paid because the company will be able to make relatively small contributions on their behalf. However, due to increasing costs of covering the entire workforce, defined benefit plans aren't as popular as they were years ago.

Raise expectations about getting richer

Suppose that Anne's company says it will give her a $10,000 raise. After the initial celebration, she may realize that more than 40% of that raise will go to federal, state and local income taxes.

Instead, Anne can ask her company to give her the raise under a special low-tax provision in the tax code: an unfunded, non-qualified deferred-compensation arrangement. The company gives her an unsecured promise to pay her in the future, with interest. This amount won't be included in Anne's gross income, so she won't owe current income taxes (however, Social Security and Medicare taxes may be due). Even if the employer sets aside a reserve to help meet this future obligation, she won't be taxed. Such plans don't "qualify" for tax deductions, so they're allowed to be skewed in favor of business owners and highly compensated employees.

Later, when Anne receives the money, she'll owe income taxes and the company can take a deduction. If she waits until retirement, she may be in a lower tax bracket. Combining that advantage with the years of tax-free compounding, she may wind up far richer than if she'd taken the raise in cash and paid her taxes right away.

Caution: You should be aware of certain rules recently imposed under the American Jobs Creation Act of 2004 for nonqualified deferred-compensation arrangements. Review and revise deferred-comp plans with your tax pro to take into account formal elections that are now required under law.

Make deductions stand up to IRS scrutiny

The IRS has announced that it's reinstating random audits of taxpayers. Although the chances of being audited are still relatively small, if you are tapped by the IRS, you can make the experience less traumatic and less expensive.

By all means, be cooperative with the examining agent, but don't overdo it. You should bring only those records you will need and confine your answers to the questions raised. Otherwise, you may open the door to new issues.

In fact, you may be better off skipping the audit altogether and have your tax adviser represent you. That way, you're not likely to speak out of turn.

When it comes to making deductions stand up in an audit, nothing beats good records. You should hold onto every scrap of paper that might be relevant for at least three years after you file a return.

What if your records aren't thorough? Reconstruct them as best you can. For example, you may be able to get old credit card statements from credit card companies and signed statements from business associates whom you visited or entertained.

Naturally, you'll want to work with a tax

pro if the IRS questions any of your deductions. Better yet, work with him from the beginning when you implement any of our tax-freeze strategies. Working together to aggressively use all legal tax-reduction strategies, the two of you can cut your taxes without running afoul of the IRS.

How to use Roth IRAs as estate-planning vehicles

The "garden variety" reason for converting a traditional IRA into a Roth account is to earn tax-free income that will be withdrawn after age 59½ to help finance your retirement years. But if you won't need the money in your IRA, converting offers another less-publicized advantage. If you intend to pass along as much as possible to your children, a Roth account can be a great estate-planning vehicle.

Don't misunderstand. Roth IRAs aren't exempt from the federal estate tax. However, by paying the upfront conversion tax, you're effectively prepaying future income taxes that would be owed by your heirs and reducing the taxable estate. And this can be done without owing any gift tax or using up any portion of the valuable estate tax exemption.

Now here's where it gets really interesting. A big advantage for Roths: They're not covered by the minimum withdrawal rules that apply to traditional IRAs. These rules force participants to begin liquidating the IRA the year after they turn 70½. Of course, this means Uncle Sam takes his cut, and the state tax collector as well. When you don't need the money, being forced to take these withdrawals and pay the resulting taxes is aggravating.

The good news: Converting a traditional IRA into a Roth account stops this nonsense in its tracks. Now you're free to leave the account balance untouched and accumulate as many tax-free dollars as possible to pass along to your heirs. (If a taxpayer is age 70½ or older, she will still have to take one final minimum withdrawal for the year of the conversion; the remaining IRA balance can then be switched to Roth status.)

Unfortunately, the minimum withdrawal exemption ends when the Roth account holder dies. Now the account falls under the same minimum withdrawal rules as regular IRAs. However, if your heirs are disciplined enough to take only their minimum required withdrawals, they may be able to string out that liquidation process for many years.

Note, however, that these favorable rules have been complicated by the SECURE Act. Under the SECURE Act, effective on January 1, 2020, nonspousal beneficiaries must take distributions within 10 years of the owner's death unless a special exception applies. The exceptions are available for distributions to individuals who are not more than 10 years younger than the owner, disabled or chronically ill individuals, or children of the owner who have not reached the age of majority. Prior arrangements involving nonspousal beneficiaries are grandfathered.

Roth IRAs are also subject to the SECURE Act crackdown, but future payouts are generally exempt from tax. Thus, there is a greater incentive to convert a traditional IRA to a Roth IRA after 2019.

As we said earlier, beginning in 2011, you can convert a traditional IRA to a Roth IRA regardless of the amount of your AGI.

For conversions in 2010, you could spread the resulting tax over the following two years, but this tax deferral is no longer available. Nevertheless, depending on your circumstances, a conversion may be a sound approach.

Final point: Previously, you could undo a Roth IRA conversion by recharacterizing the Roth back into a traditional IRA by the tax return due date for the year of the conversion, plus extensions. For instance, you might want to recharacterize should the value of the account drops to avoid overpaying tax on the conversion. But the TCJA repeals this technique, beginning in 2018.

Made in the USA
Monee, IL
28 January 2020

x.net